Interlaced

InterLaced

Poems & Devotions
of Love, Life & Faith

ELDORA
VETTER

Elkhorn, Nebraska USA

Unless otherwise noted, scripture quotations are taken from the New International Version of the Bible. Throughout the book, versions of the Bible used are:

New International Version (NIV)

The New King James Version (NKJV)

King James Version (KJV)

The Living Bible Paraphrased (TLBP)

Unless indicated, all photos are supplied from the personal collections of Eldora Vetter, with permission granted from either the subjects or the photographer, where required.

ISBN10: 0-9842819-1-6

ISBN13: 978-0-9842819-1-6

Library of Congress Control Number: 2010934179

Printed in The United States

10 9 8 7 6 5 4 3 2 1

To my husband, Jack,
who is a constant encouragement to me.

To my children, Denny, Vicki and Todd
and their spouses who bring joy to my life.

To my grandchildren and great-grandchildren
who complete my life.

CONTENTS

Dedication

Acknowledgments...I

Foreword V

*I*NTRODUCTION

Sermons We See IX

A Prayer for You...XIII

Today's Prayer.. XV

*D*EVOTIONS

Giving Jesus What We Have.. 1

Yes, I Can Make a Difference (People Who Care)................... 7

A Servant's Heart 15

As We Continue to Grow.. 21

God Will Hold Me Accountable 27

If Jesus Came to Our House 33

Where Art Thou? 39

When Is It Christmas?... 55

Peace, Be Still.. 59

A Recipe for Happiness 65

God's Handfuls on Purpose 71

What Have You Done With The Gift?..................................... 79

I Don't Understand (John 3:16).. 85

Choices (The Power of Choice) 89

The Joy of Giving 97

Enough (The Refiner of Silver)... 103

The Prodigal Son Part 1: What Are You Looking For?....... 109

The Prodigal Son Part 2: The Brother 115

Family and Friends

Thank God For My Childhood 123
My Dad 133
As We Walk on Life's Way 136
Jim Mabrey Farewell Party 141
God's Gift of Friendship 143
Bernie & Susie 153
My Valentine 155
Memories 157
A Tribute to Virgle Vetter 161
Retirement 165
Thank You for 25 Years 167
Happy 50th Anniversary Les & Iloe 171
My Baby Brother 175
Dalton 181

Special Occasions/Other/Misc.

Vetters Go the Extra Mile 187
As Christmas Draws Near 190
Dime Jars 193
Pastors Are Special 194
Bernie 196
Christmas Gift Clues 197
I'll Be Your Friend 199
Especially for You… 201
Bernie & Zaiga 203
The Eighth Day! 205
Thank You! 208
For Joani 209
No Ordinary Bear 211

About the Author

About Eldora Vetter 217
Lifetime Achievement Award 219

$\mathcal{A}$CKNOWLEDGMENTS

$\mathcal{I}$give praise to Jesus, my Savior, my constant companion, my Lord and my friend.

Thank you to Glenna Arent, my sister-in-law, who condensed my outlines into devotions suitable for this book.

DaNita Naimoli, you have been my mentor, my advisor and friend as we tackled this project together, and I thank you for your patience and guidance.

Joani Schelm, for being such a friend and big part of my life through the years. For your love and support always.

Julie Knobbe, for your assistance, love and support.

The Vetter Health Services (VHS) administrators and staff have often asked me to gather my work into a book to use in the nursing homes, and this book is the result of that prompting.

My extended family, friends and the Vetter Health Services Team who continue to inspire me.

Psalm 25:4–5 (NIV)

Show me your ways, O Lord, teach me your paths; guide me in your truth and teach me, for you are my God, my Savior, and my hope is in you all day long.

$\mathscr{F}$OREWORD

BY JOANI SCHELM

$\mathscr{O}$ne of the most precious gifts God placed in my life was giving me Eldora as a sister-in-law. She brings such joy to my life and to the lives of our families. Her smile, her laughter, her love…are faithfully delivered with a sincere warm hug.

My earliest vivid memory of Eldora was when I was six years old; she and my mother were meticulously sewing rows of tiny pearl buttons on her shiny satin wedding dress. I had never seen such a gorgeous dress or bride. Little did I know the many *pearls of wisdom* she would bring to my life in future years.

Eldora is a remarkable woman who by example has taught me lots of lessons over the years. Life lessons like how to prepare and serve an attractive meal, how to stretch a dollar a long ways, how to raise my children and grandchildren… reminding me that they grow up too fast, and to be thankful for each new day.

Eldora's poems flow from her heart; they inspire us. The messages are filled with wisdom, hope, humility, and humor. They challenge us; they speak of possibilities, of strength, peace and love...love of family; the value of friendship; the joy of giving.

As you read this book, you will see that Eldora's true beauty is her loving heart. Her life is an example of God's love. She doesn't put God in first place; she puts him every place.

I pray Eldora's message through poetry will bless your life just a fraction of how she has influenced me.

Enjoy!

INTRODUCTION

̄SERMONS WE SEE

This poem was sent to me in 1952 by my cousin who was serving in the military. I have always loved this poem and it was probably one of the things that inspired me to start writing poetry. It's as true today as it was the day I received it. I still dig it out to read it or use it once in a while in a devotion.

ᵉᶜ SERMONS WE SEE ᵒᵇ
—EDGAR GUEST

I'd rather see a sermon than to hear one any day;
I'd rather one should walk with me than merely tell the way.
The eye's a better pupil and more willing than the ear;
Fine council is confusing, but example's always clear;
And the best of all the preachers are the men who live their creeds,
For to see good put in action is what everybody needs.

I soon can learn to do it if you'll let me see it done;
I can watch your hands in action, but your tongue too fast may run.
And the lecture you deliver may be very wise and true;
But I'd rather get my lessons by observing what you do.
For I might misunderstand you and the high advice you give,
But there's no misunderstanding how you act and how you live.

When I see a deed of kindness, I am eager to be kind.
When a weaker brother stumbles and a strong man stays behind
Just to see if he can help him, then the wish grows strong in me,
To become as big and thoughtful as I know that I can be.
And all the travelers can witness that the best of guides today
Is not the one who tells you, but the one who shows the way.

One good man teaches many, men believe what they behold;
One deed of kindness noticed is worth forty that are told.
Who stands with men of honor learns to hold his honor dear,
For right living speaks a language which to everyone is clear.
Though an able speaker charms me with his eloquence, I say,
I'd rather see a sermon than to hear one, any day.

Eldora and Jack Vetter, 1957

$\mathscr{A}$ Prayer For You

This poem was written in my Bible that Jack took to France with him when he was deployed in September 1957. It was penned during his 30-day furlough when we learned we were pregnant with our first son, Denith Dean.

This is the only poem, of several written for him (Jack), that I still have today.

Each day I'll breathe a prayer and say
Lord each moment of the day
Keep him safe while he's away
And bring him back to me to stay!

Lord as he walks the path with you
Keep him faithful—keep him true
That he might live in light divine
Just let his will be wholly thine.

That he would trust you for your grace
When trials would meet him face to face,
That he might live each day for you
Because your grace will see him through.

Now Lord I give him to your care
Because I know you answer prayer,
Help him a faithful witness be
Until your blessed face we see.

TODAY'S PRAYER

GOD'S TRAINING GROUND

*I*n the book of Exodus we find the story of a tiny baby boy who was lovingly placed in a basket by his Hebrew mother and hidden in the reeds along the river bank. This baby would change the destiny of a whole nation.

One day, Pharaoh's daughter was bathing in the river when a baby's cry was heard. The basket was found and the baby discovered. She took the baby into the palace, named him Moses, and accepted him as her son. He was raised with all of the privileges of royalty, but deep in his heart the seed of love for his people that had been planted began to grow.

There were times when he was torn between his comfortable life in the palace and seeing how his own people were treated. Eventually that frustration resulted in Moses killing an Egyptian man who was mistreating a Hebrew worker, and he had to flee to the desert to make a new life for himself. It was in the desert that Moses recognized God's voice, and at about eighty years of age he became the man that would lead his people out of Egypt. God had a plan and he chose Moses to carry out that plan.

Sometimes we may think that we have our lives all planned out, but God may have a different plan for us. Perhaps the loss of a job or illness may cause an abrupt change in our plans. Like Moses, we may find ourselves in the "desert" of life wondering what decisions we should make or what direction we should go. God doesn't want us to remain in the desert place. If we put our trust in him and listen for his voice, he will help us to find the plan that he has for our lives.

Moses faced many tests and trials as he led the Children of Israel out of Egypt. The people soon forgot the hardships that they had suffered. They griped about the food that God provided for them each day because there was not enough variety. They complained that there wasn't fresh water to drink. Moses took their complaints to God and God met their need and provided for them. Moses didn't have a GPS or a map to find his way across the desert. He talked to God; God met the need and provided a cloud by day and a pillar of fire by night to direct the way. Not only was Moses responsible for the physical needs of the people, he was also their spiritual leader. The burden was heavy but God met the need and provided the Ten Commandments written on tablets of stone. Moses learned complete trust in God to meet any need.

There may be times in our lives when we feel as though we are wandering in the desert without much guidance or control. There may even be times when we're not sure where the money will come from to pay the bills or maybe even to be able to buy food for our family. There are times when we have to put our total faith in God; do our part and trust him to answer prayer and provide for our needs.

Trusting is not always easy, but as we seek to know God, we find that he can be relied on to lead and guide us through all the tests and trials of life that might come our way.

Do you trust God to meet your needs?

Eldora and Jack Vetter, 2009

TODAY'S PRAYER

Written in October 2005, for our Vetter Health Services (VHS) 30th Anniversary celebration as a time of reflection over the past thirty years. Forty-eight years have gone by and this is how I would rewrite the poem that was in the back of the Bible!

Today I'll breathe a prayer for you
For all the things that you must do,
The big decisions that come your way—
Dear Lord: "Please walk with him today."

Lord, as he lives today for you,
Give him strength and wisdom too;
Help us to live in light divine,
Just help our wills be wholly Thine.

That we will trust you for your grace
When problems meet us face to face,
Help us each day to trust in you
Because your love will see us through.

Dear Lord, just keep us in your care
Because we know you answer prayer,
Help us, your servants, to do your will,
Let us hear you whisper, "Peace, be Still."

DEVOTIONS

GIVING JESUS WHAT WE HAVE

JESUS FEEDS THE 5,000 WITH A SMALL BOY'S LUNCH

MATTHEW 14:13–15 *When Jesus heard what had happened, he withdrew by boat privately to a solitary place. Hearing of this, the crowds followed him on foot from the towns. When Jesus landed and saw the large crowd, he had compassion on them and healed their sick.*

As evening approached, the disciples came to him and said, "This is a remote place, and it's already getting late. Send the crowds away, so they can go to the villages and buy themselves some food."

JOHN 6:5–13 *When Jesus looked up and saw a great crowd coming toward him, he said to Phillip, "Where shall we buy bread for these* people to eat?" He asked this only to test him, for he already had in mind what he was going to do.

Phillip answered him, "Eight months' wages would not buy enough bread for each one to have a bite!"

Another of his disciples, Andrew, Simon Peter's brother, spoke up, "Here is a boy with five small barley loaves and two small fish, but how far will they go among so many?"

Jesus said, "Have the people sit down." There was plenty of grass in that place, and the men sat down, about five thousand of them. Jesus then took the loaves, gave thanks, and distributed to those who were seated as much as they wanted. He did the same with the fish.

When they had all had enough to eat, he said to his disciples, "Gather the pieces that are left over, Let nothing be wasted." So they gathered them and filled twelve baskets with pieces of the five barley loaves left over by those who had eaten.

*J*esus had spent the day ministering to his followers. A large group of pilgrims on their way to Jerusalem to celebrate the annual Passover had followed him all day, watching him heal the sick. Late in the evening, Jesus and his disciples climbed a hill along the shore of the Sea of Galilee and sat down to rest. Before long, a great multitude of people began to climb the hill looking for Jesus, and the disciples realized they had a problem on their hands.

The crowd was hungry, there was not enough money to purchase food and there were no McDonald's nearby. One alternative was to send the people on their way. Andrew, one of the disciples, had scouted out the crowd and had found a small lad willing to give the lunch that his mother had packed for him. Jesus took the five barley loaves and the two fish; gave thanks (a great example to follow) and began to multiply the food. The story in the Gospel of John recounts that 5,000 men plus women and children ate until they were full and there were twelve baskets of leftovers!

This miracle was the result of teamwork. Jesus saw the need and had compassion on the crowd. The disciples did their part to solve the problem by scouting out the crowd and locating the lad with the lunch. The small lad willingly gave all he had to eat and then Jesus multiplied the food until there was plenty for all.

The scripture doesn't tell us if there were other people in the crowd that day who might have had some food that they could have shared with others. Perhaps there were those who chose not to share what they had and because of that choice missed out on being part of the miracle. Galatians 6:9-10 says, "And let us not get tired of doing what is right, for after a while we will reap a harvest of blessing if we don't get discouraged and give up. That's why we should always be kind to everyone, and especially to our Christian brothers."

There are people all around us who are in need. Some are in need of the most basic necessities of food, shelter and clothing; others may have a temporary need. Still others are in need of an introduction to the Savior. We can all do our part to meet someone's needs.

"If you can't feed a hundred people, then feed just one."
—*author unknown*

Would you ask God to help you be sensitive to the needs of those around you?

GIVING JESUS WHAT WE HAVE

What if Jesus had said,
"This has been a long day,
Go meet that crowd
And send them away."?

What if the mother
had not planned ahead
And knew that her young son
Would need to be fed?

What if the lad
Had not given his lunch
When the survey was taken
Of the food for that bunch?

What if the crowd
Were not willing to stay?
They were tired and hungry
It was late in the day.

What if the disciples
Had not followed the plan
To carefully group
And seat every man?

They would have missed a great blessing,
And so would have we,
Often the best things
Are the ones we can't see.

Jesus asks only
We give what we can,
Often the little things
Will fit right in his plan;

We must all work together,
Each one doing their part,
"Whatsoever your hands find,
Do with all of your heart."

*Y*es, I Can Make A Difference
(People Who Care)

The story of "Naaman the Leper" and the people who cared

2 Kings 5:1–14 *Now Naaman was commander of the army of the king of Aram. He was a great man in the sight of his master and highly regarded, because through him the Lord had given victory to Aram. He was a valiant soldier, but he had leprosy.*

Now bands from Aram had gone out and had taken captive a young girl from Israel and she served Naaman's wife. She said to her mistress, "If only my master would see the prophet who is in Samaria! He would cure him of his leprosy."

Naaman went to his master and told him what the girl from Israel had said, "By all means, go," the king of Aram replied. "I will send a letter to the king of Israel." So Naaman left, taking with him ten talents of silver, six thousand shekels of gold and ten sets of clothing. The letter that he took to the king of Israel read: "With this letter I am sending my servant Naaman to you so that you may cure him of his leprosy."

As soon as the king of Israel read the letter, he tore his robes and said, "Am I God?" Can I kill and bring back to life? Why does this fellow send someone to me to be cured of his leprosy? See how he is trying to pick a quarrel with me?"

When Elisha the man of God heard that the king of Israel had torn his robes, he sent him this message: "Why have you torn your robes? Have the man come to me and he will know that there is a prophet in Israel." So Naaman went with his horses and chariots and stopped at the door of Elisha's house. Elisha sent a messenger to say to him, "Go, wash yourself seven times in the Jordan, and your flesh will be restored and you will be cleansed."

But Naaman went away angry and said, "I thought that he would surely come out to me and stand and call on the name of the Lord his God, wave his hand over the spot and cure me of my leprosy. Are not Abana and Pharpar, the rivers of Damascus, better than any of the *waters of Israel? Couldn't I wash in them and be cleansed?" So he turned and went off in a rage.*

Naaman's servants went to him and said, "My father, if the prophet had told you to do some great thing, would you not have done it? How much more, then, when he tells you, 'Wash and be cleansed!'" So he went down and dipped himself in the Jordan seven times, as the man of God had told him, and his flesh was restored and became clean like that of a young boy.

A little girl was kidnapped from Israel and taken to the country of Syria to become a servant to Naaman's wife. Apparently she had been taught to have faith and to care about others. Her master, Naaman was the commander-in-chief of the great army of the King of Syria and suffered from leprosy. The servant girl's heart was filled with compassion for him, and she told him that he should seek healing from the prophet in Samaria.

When the King of Syria heard about this, he wrote a letter of recommendation for Naaman and had expensive gifts gathered to present to the King of Israel. He encouraged Naaman to make the journey, and so Naaman and his soldiers traveled to meet the King. The King of Israel had no idea how to provide a cure for Naaman and suspected that some type of plot was underway to capture him and his people.

The prophet Elisha was a man of God, and when he heard about all of this, he sent a message to Naaman that he would be cured of the leprosy once he dipped into the river Jordan seven times. Naaman had expected that Elisha would perform a spectacular, instant miracle for all to see and was humiliated and furious with the message to dip into the Jordan River. He let his pride rule and was ready to head for home and forget about being healed.

Naaman was highly regarded among his soldiers, and they truly cared about him. They came up with a plan to talk him into trying what Elisha had told him to do. Fortunately, Naaman was willing to listen to his soldiers and follow the instructions that Elisha had given to him. He dipped himself in the Jordan River and, after the seventh time, his skin was cleared of the disease. Naaman recognized that his healing did not come from the river water but was the result of the healing power of the one true God. His life was changed forever from the inside out!

This story is a good example of people who cared enough to become involved in someone else's life. The young girl could have been bitter to have been taken from her home and forced to be a servant in a foreign country; instead, she showed compassion. Naaman had served his King well, and in return the King went out of his way to help him. Elisha listened to God and followed his leading. The soldiers respected their leader and were not afraid to reason with him. Each person had a part to play, and their decisions could have changed the outcome of this story.

Do you care enough about people to risk
being part of their lives?

✌ YES, I CAN ✌
MAKE A DIFFERENCE
(PEOPLE WHO CARE)

Now she was a captive
In a far away land,
But she gave her life freely
Into God's hand.

The facts of this story
Would not be here today
If the pride of the servant girl
Had gotten in her way.

"I can make a difference!
As I serve Naaman's wife,
I can show God's goodness
Each day of my life."

Now as we look at Naaman,
A great man was he,
He was willing to listen
To his servants, you see.

A word softly spoken
Without fanfare or show;
Because of this servant girl,
Naaman was willing to go.

Naaman was desperate
As he went to the king,
A cure for his leprosy
Was no common thing!

The king, he was willing
To give it a try,
He could have let Naaman
Just stay home and die

He sent great possessions
And a letter to tell
To the great king of Israel,
"Just make Naaman well."

Now, the king of Israel
Just could not understand
Why the king of Aram
Would make this demand;

Surely this is a trick,
The demand was too great,
He could not cure Naaman
Of this leprosy state.

When the news reached Elisha
Of the king's great distress,
He sent word to the king
He'd put his God to the test!

From the door of the prophet,
The message went out,
It made Naaman angry!
And he left in a pout.

I can just hear the servants
As they all drove away—
Do we dare to let Naaman
Go home this way?

Again they reasoned with Naaman
As they went on their way,
"You'd better consider
What the prophet did say."

"If a great thing were required,
You'd somehow find a way
To do whatever was asked
By the prophet today."

Again Naaman would listen to
What his servants would say,
After swallowing his pride
He did things God's way.

One thing in this lesson
We surely can see:
The best things in life
Most often are free!

Down to the Jordan,
He'd give it a try,
The other alternative
Was to go home and die.

Seven dips in the Jordan
Is what he would do!
The seventh time he came up,
His skin was brand new!

What if one person
had failed in their task
or had simply refused
to have done what God asked?

Things would have been different,
The news would have read
On the back page in fine print:
"Naaman the leper is dead."

This story of triumph,
Today we have shared,
Not really about Naaman
But about people who cared.

A Servant's Heart

The story of Jesus, taking a servant's role, and washing his disciples' feet...

JOHN 13:1–17 *It was just before the Passover Feast. Jesus knew that the time had come for him to leave this world and go to the Father. Having loved his own who were in the world; he now showed them the full extent of his love.*

The evening meal was being served, and the devil had already prompted Judas Iscariot, son of Simon, to betray Jesus. Jesus knew that the Father had put all things under his power, and that he had come from God and was returning to God: so he got up from the meal, took off his outer clothing, and wrapped a towel around his waist. After that, he poured water into a basin and began to wash his disciples' feet, drying them with the towel that was wrapped around him.

He came to Simon Peter, who said to him, "Lord, are you going to wash my feet?"

Jesus replied, "You do not realize now what I am doing, but later you will understand."

"No," said Peter, "you shall never wash my feet."

Jesus answered, "Unless I wash you, you have no part with me."

"Then, Lord," Simon Peter replied, "not just my feet but my hands and my head as well!"

Jesus answered, "A person who has had a bath needs only to wash his feet: his whole body is clean. And you are clean, though not every one of you." For he knew who was going to betray him, and that was why he said not every one was clean.

When he had finished washing their feet, he put on his clothes and returned to his place. "Do you understand what I have done for you?" he asked them. "You call me 'Teacher' and 'Lord' and rightly so, for that is what I am. Now that I, your Lord and Teacher have washed your feet you also should wash one another's feet. I have set you an example that you should do as I have done for you. I tell you the truth, no servant is greater than his master, nor is a messenger greater than the one who sent him. Now that you know these things, you will be blessed if you do them."

There were no airplanes, buses, cars or even paved roads when Jesus lived on earth. People walked from place to place on dusty roads, and it was the custom of the day for servants to wash the feet of the guests when they arrived. In John's Gospel chapter 13:1–17, we find the story of Jesus assuming the role of a servant as he washed and dried the feet of his disciples just before the Passover Feast.

The disciples knew Jesus as teacher and Lord and felt that it was beneath him to wash their feet. They were a bit unnerved that he would serve them. Jesus washed and dried their feet as an act of love toward them, but he also used this time to share with them the importance of ministering to each other.

One of the first words a small child learns to say is "me," and our society makes it quite easy to continue that way of thinking into our adult lives. However, that lifestyle creates very self-centered and unfulfilled people. It's important that we learn to put others before ourselves.

It is far more rewarding to follow the example that Jesus set of serving others.

Is there someone that you could serve and minister to today?

A SERVANT'S HEART

Oh, dare I ask
For a servant's heart?
Am I really willing
To do my part?

Am I willing to go
That extra mile?
When things are rough,
Can I wear a smile?

Am I really willing
To bow my knee
And meet the needs
Of those I see?

To give of myself
When no one's there
To see my deeds
Or hear my prayer?

When I bow down
To tie a shoe,
Will I take the time
To minister too?

Can I put away
All false pretense
And not always stand
In my own defense?

My heart's not really
What you all see,
It's what I am
When I'm alone with me.

Lord help me always
To do my part,
Create in me
A servant's heart.

$\mathcal{A}$s We Continue
to Grow

Accounts of spiritual growth

2 Peter 1:3–11 *His divine power has given us everything we need for life and godliness through our knowledge of him who called us by his own glory and goodness. Through these he has given us his very great and precious promises, so that through them you may participate in the divine nature and escape the corruption in the world caused by evil desires.*

For this very reason, make every effort to add to your faith goodness; and to goodness, knowledge; and to knowledge, self-control; and to self-control, perseverance; and to perseverance, godliness; and to godliness, brotherly kindness; and to brotherly kindness, love. For if you possess these qualities in increasing measure, they will keep you from being ineffective and unproductive in your knowledge of our Lord Jesus Christ. But if anyone does not have them, he is nearsighted and blind, and has forgotten that he has been cleansed from his past sins.

Therefore, my brothers, be all the more eager to make your calling and election sure. For if you do these things, you will never fall, and you will receive a rich welcome into the eternal kingdom of our Lord and Savior Jesus Christ.

2 PETER 3:17–18 *Therefore, dear friends, since you already know this, be on your guard so that you may not be carried away by the error of lawless men and fall from your secure position. But grow in the grace and knowledge of our Lord and Savior Jesus Christ. To him be glory both now and forever! Amen.*

Milk provides the vitamins and nutrients that a baby needs for the first several months of life, but a variety of nutritious food is necessary for the child to continue to grow and develop. Many components combine to meet specific needs for strong, healthy bodies and sound minds. Their minds and personalities develop as they watch the lives of those around them, advance through the educational system, and experience all the ups and downs of life.

Spiritual growth can be compared to the growth and maturity of human minds and bodies. Hebrews 5:13–14 puts it something like this: "For everyone who continues to feed on milk is obviously inexperienced, unskilled in the doctrine of righteousness (of conformity to the divine Will in purpose, thought and action), for he is a mere infant [not able to talk yet]! But solid food is for full-grown men, for those whose senses and mental faculties are trained by practice to discriminate and distinguish between what is morally good and noble and what is evil and contrary either to divine or human law." The instruction continues: "Therefore, let us go on and get past the elementary stage in the teachings and doctrine of Christ (the Messiah), advancing steadily toward the completeness and perfection that belongs to spiritual mentality."

It is not God's desire for us to remain as spiritual babies. Spiritual growth involves various dimensions. The first step is to acknowledge Jesus as Lord and Savior and to align our lives to God's plan for us. Continual spiritual growth is dependent on studying God's word, prayer, and developing a personal relationship with him. God invites us to be part of his team. If we do our part, he will be faithful to guide us on our path to spiritual maturity.

Have you made the decision to be part of God's team?

⋖ AS WE CONTINUE ⋗ TO GROW

As we ponder the subject we all need to know—
Has our faith become stagnant, does it continue to grow?

When we were all children, it was easy to say
That God up in Heaven would take care of each day.

Then as we grew older through high school or college,
We knew we'd arrived, we had a diploma and knowledge.

Then we suddenly found ourselves out on our own
And no one could tell us we weren't fully grown.

We soon learned one lesson as we continued to grow—
There were a good many things we still didn't know.

We were sure that the answer for the rest of our life
Would all fall into place when we became husband and wife.

When the children arrived, life took on a new turn—
The right and the wrong, each day they must learn.

We suddenly knew we needed some help,
We now were responsible for more than our self.

The challenge we're given—whatever the task—
There's help from above, we just have to ask.

There's good and there's bad with each new day we face.
But there are great opportunities to grow in God's grace.

Now all of the answers we never will know,
But we must keep on learning even when it seems slow.

As we face the future, whether we reap or we sow,
It's truly from God that we continue to grow.

This poem was written in the fall of 1992, riding on a bus from the airport to the Administrators' Conference in Georgia. The theme of the conference was "Vetter Health Services (VHS) Grows Quality—Come Grow With Us."

ᎶOD WILL HOLD ME ACCOUNTABLE

GIVING AN ACCOUNT FOR THE TALENTS EACH OF US WAS GIVEN

MATTHEW 25:14–30 *Again, it will be like a man going on a journey, who called his servants and entrusted his property to them. To one he gave five talents of money, to another two talents, and to another one talent, each according to his ability. Then he went on his journey. The man who had received the five talents went at once and put his money to work and gained five more. So also, the one with the two talents gained two more. But the man who had received the one talent went off, dug a hole in the ground and hid his master's money.*

After a long time the master of those servants returned and settled accounts with them. The man who had received the five talents brought the other five. "Master," he said, "you entrusted me with five talents. See, I have gained five more."

His master replied, "Well done, good and faithful servant! You have been faithful with a few things: I will put you in charge of many things. Come and share your master's happiness!"

The man with the two talents also came. "Master," he said, "you entrusted me with two talents; see, I have gained two more."

His master replied, "Well done, good and faithful servant! You have been faithful with a few things: I will put you in charge of many things. Come and share your master's happiness!"

Then the man who had received the one talent came. "Master," he said, "I knew that you are a hard man, harvesting where you have not sown and gathering where you have not scattered seed. So I was afraid and went out and hid your talent in the ground. See, here is what belongs to you."

His master replied, "You wicked, lazy servant! So you knew that I harvest where I have not sown and gather where I have not scattered seed? Well then, you should have put my money on deposit with the bankers, so that when I returned I would have received it back with interest."

"Take the talent from him and give it to the one who has the ten talents. For everyone who has will be given more and he will have abundance. Whoever does not have, even what he has will be taken from him. And throw the worthless servant outside, into the darkness, where there will be weeping and gnashing of teeth."

*J*esus used parables to illustrate life lessons. In Matthew, chapter 25, we find the parable of a rich nobleman who divided up his wealth among three of his trusted servants and left the country for an extended period of time. One servant received five talents (worth approximately $5,000 today); another received two talents; and the third received one talent. Their master did not conduct training seminars or provide reference manuals on how his money should be managed during his absence.

Communication was nearly impossible as cell phones and internet service were not available, and he was not able to check with his servants to see how things were going at home. The day finally came when he returned home and the servants were required to give an account of the money they were in charge of. The servant with the five talents had used wisdom and skills to double the money. The second servant had also made wise choices and doubled the two talents he had been given. These servants received rich rewards for their faithful service. The third servant had hidden the money away. He had only the original amount to present to his master and as a consequence suffered his master's wrath.

The world's view of accountability often is one of "passing the buck" or blaming someone else for our actions. Sometimes it may be difficult to own up to our lapse of integrity, our lack of compassion for those less fortunate, or our willful disobedience to God. One day God will require an account of the talents, time, resources and opportunities that we have been given to serve him.

He doesn't expect us to be able to accomplish everything on our own. In Hebrews 13:5 God tells us, "I will not in any way fail you nor give you up or leave you without support." He has left us clear instructions in his complete reference manual, the Bible. It contains examples for us to follow—the dos, don'ts and how tos—and his expectations for us and the rewards that are ours when those expectations are met.

Are you living your life according to God's guidelines of accountability?

GOD WILL HOLD ME ACCOUNTABLE

God will hold me accountable, this one thing I know,
For the things that I do, and the places I go.

He'll hold me accountable for the things that I say,
For my every thought and my attitude each day.

To train up my children in the way they should go
So when they're adults, God's word they will know.

To provide for my family, a job I can't shirk,
An honest day's pay for an honest day's work.

I must give to the poor and look out for my brother.
I must honor my spouse and my father and mother.

The money I earn, God knows the amount,
What I do with it, I'll give an account.

He'll hold me accountable for the lies that I tell—
Even though I think I've covered them well.

The sins done in secret, whether big or real small,
When God's books are open, I'll account for them all.

The sins of omission, things he asked me to do,
I was too busy—I'll account for that too.

We'll all be accountable for the vows that we take,
For the debts that we owe and the promises we break.

Then there's the talents! We'll account for them too—
If we had many, or only a few.

We'll be held accountable for our weaker brother—
To rescue, to help and to uplift each other.

When we think of the things we're accountable for,
All the things we have listed, and a good many more.

To be accountable for all we can't do by ourselves,
And that is the reason we need the Lord's help.

All added together, it's a tremendous amount—
Still, for life's greatest question, we must give an account.

In all of God's plan, he made us a way—
What will we do with Jesus today?

God sent us a Savior, his blood covers our sin,
If we open our heart he'll be glad to come in.

He'll stay right here with us, stay close by our side,
If we've only one talent, we don't have to hide.

He'll take that one talent and bless it real good,
Then we can do more than we thought that we could.

Is Jesus your lord? In your life, is he part?
He's the only provision for an acceptable heart!

$\mathcal{I}$f Jesus Came To Our House

Story of Jesus stopping by Mary and Martha's home. What would you do if he came to your home?

Luke 10:38–42 *As Jesus and his disciples were on their way, he came to a village where a woman named Martha opened her home to him. She had a sister called Mary, who sat at the Lord's feet listening to what he said. But Martha was distracted by all the preparations that had to be made. She came to him and asked, "Lord, don't you care that my sister has left me to do the work by myself? Tell her to help me!"*

"Martha, Martha," the Lord answered, "you are worried and upset about many things, but only one thing is needed. Mary has chosen what is better, and it will not be taken away from her."

$\mathcal{C}$ompany has arrived! Many things need to be done. The house and guest rooms need to be freshened up and preparations made for a meal! By the time the company is greeted and settled in, the hostess may be too anxious to even enjoy the guests. Does this sound familiar to you?

Jesus was a welcome guest in the home of Mary and Martha at anytime, and they looked forward with great anticipation to his visits. Jesus and his disciples were passing by and stopped in for a visit. In a short while, Jesus began to share and to teach. Mary sat at Jesus' feet and listened intently as she allowed his teaching to minister to her. Meanwhile, Martha was concerned about getting the dinner meal completed by herself. She became a bit troubled and overwhelmed with all there was to do and asked Jesus to tell Mary to come and help with the preparations.

Jesus gently reminded Martha that she should not be so anxious and worried about things of temporary value but that her greatest desire should be his teaching which had eternal value. Mary's spirit longed for closeness to Jesus, and she was willing to lay everything aside to spend time listening to his teaching. Martha's intentions were good in her desire to serve Jesus, but she allowed herself to be overly concerned with details and all that she thought that she needed to do. She missed out on the best part of the evening.

We can get so caught up in details that we don't enjoy the special times. We need to guard ourselves so that our busyness doesn't crowd out the importance of spending time with Jesus each day. He wants to be welcomed into our lives. He longs for us to seek him and to fellowship with him.

Are you overwhelmed with the routine
of daily life, or do you quiet yourself before
Jesus each day and allow him to minister
to your heart?

⸙ IF JESUS ⸙
CAME TO OUR HOUSE

If Jesus came to our house to spend a day or two,
If he came unexpectedly, I wonder what we'd do?

Oh! We'd give him the nicest room he's such an honored guest,
And all the food we'd serve him would be the very best.

And we'd keep assuring him we were glad to have him there,
That serving him right in our home was joy beyond compare!

But when we saw him coming, would we meet him at the door
With arms outstretched in welcome to our heavenly visitor?

Or would we be so busy as we saw him standing there
That we'd ask him to come back when we had time to spare?

Or would we need to change our clothes before we let him in?
Hide the books and magazines, put the Bible where they'd been?

Would we turn off the radio and hope he hadn't heard,
And wish we hadn't uttered that last loud or ugly word?

Would we hide our worldly music and put our hymn books out,
Could we let Jesus right in or would we need to rush about?

And I wonder, if the Savior came to spend a day or two,
Would we just keep on doing the things we always do?

Would we go right on saying the things we always say?
Would life for us continue as it does from day to day?

Would our family conversation keep up with its usual pace?
Would we find it hard to sit down and say the table grace?

If Jesus stood beside us as we tucked our child in bed,
Would we be more careful that our evening prayers were said?

Would we sing the songs we sing and read the books we read
And let him know on which of these our mind and spirit feed?

Would Jesus be real pleased with the way we treat our spouse?
Would the atmosphere be such he'd feel welcome at our house?

Would we have to change the channel that our TV set is on?
Be more careful of selections 'til our honored guest was gone?

Would we be so concerned that our house was clean and neat,
That there simply wasn't any time to sit at Jesus' feet?

Or would we need to mow the lawn or read the daily news?
Or put gas in the family car and take care of honey-dos?

Would we find any time at all to sit at Jesus' feet?
Or would we be in the kitchen—fixing food to eat?

Would we take Jesus with us everywhere we planned to go?
Or would we maybe change our plans just for a day or so?

If Jesus stood there with us as we filed our income tax,
Would we be more careful how we prepared the facts?

Would we be glad to have him meet our very closest friends?
Or would we hope they'd stay away just until his visit ends?

If Jesus was out on the road and just was passing through,
Would he feel free to just stop in to spend a day or two?

Would we be glad to have him stay forever on and on?
Or would we sigh with great relief when he at last was gone?

Or would we be so busy, we'd send him on his way—
But we'd be sure and tell him to come back another day.

It might be interesting—to know what we would do—
If Jesus came in person to live with me and you?

$\mathcal{W}$HERE ART THOU?

A 5-Part Devotion and Refrain Combining Genesis 3:6–10, Exodus 3:2–10, 1 Samuel 17:45–51, Jonah 1:1–3, Acts 9:1–6

$\mathcal{A}$dam and Eve enjoyed the beautiful Garden of Eden that God had created. God walked in the garden with them and fellowshipped with them. The garden was filled with plants and trees that provided them with a bountiful variety of food. God gave them only one stipulation: they were not to eat the fruit from the tree of knowledge of good and evil.

The scriptures in Genesis tell us that Adam and Eve gave into temptation and ate the forbidden fruit. Later, God was walking in the garden and when they heard him call, "Where art thou?" they hid among the trees. Because of their disobedience, God banished them from the garden forever. They lost the precious communion with God that they had experienced.

The Old Testament's books of Samuel detail the story of David's life and how important it was to put God first in his life. He was the youngest son in the family and honed his skills as a leader and protector as he tended the family's sheep herd. One day, the prophet Samuel made a visit to the family and revealed that God had chosen the shepherd boy, David, as the future King of Israel. David was willing to submit himself to God's timing and his plan for his life.

The Israeli army was at war with the Philistine army, and for forty days the giant, Goliath, had made threats to destroy and capture the Israelites. Although David was still just a boy, he had learned to trust God; and knowing that God would be with him, he didn't hesitate to face Goliath. David ran toward the giant with his slingshot, and with God's help he killed Goliath with a single stone.

David experienced many highs and lows during the forty years that he reigned as King of Israel. He wasn't perfect, and he committed grievous sins, but he loved God, sincerely repented of his sins, asked for forgiveness, and accepted God's chastisement and correction. David's love for God is reflected in the Book of Psalms.

David's heart for God is an example for us to follow. He committed himself to fulfill God's purpose for his life. He prepared himself to carry out God's plan and accepted the challenges along the way. He desired to be a good leader and sought God for direction. He sincerely loved God with all his heart and was quick to repent of his sins.

If you heard God's voice calling,
"Where art thou?" would you hide as Adam
and Eve did, or would you follow David's
example and submit to God's purpose for
your life?

WHERE ART THOU?
ADAM AND EVE

WHERE ARE YOU WHEN YOU'VE SINNED?

GENESIS 3:6–10 *When the woman saw that the fruit of the tree was good for food and pleasing to the eye, and also desirable for gaining wisdom, she took some and ate it. She also gave some to her husband, who was with her, and he ate it. Then the eyes of both of them were opened and they realized they were naked: so they sewed fig leaves together and made covering for themselves.*

Then the man and his wife heard the sound of the Lord God as he was walking in the garden in the cool of the day, and they hid from the Lord God among the trees of the garden. But the Lord God called to the man, "Where are you?"

He answered, "I heard you in the garden, and I was afraid because I was naked; so I hid."

WHERE ART THOU?
ADAM AND EVE

Where art thou, Adam?
Was God's question that day,
And he couldn't escape,
Though, try as he may.

Where art thou, Adam?
It was the cool of the day,
And Adam and Eve
Had hidden away.

They had sewn fig leaves
To cover their skin,
But really had hoped
It would cover their sin.

"It was this woman you gave me—
That you took from my side,"
To admit they had sinned
Was too much for their pride.

𝒲HERE ART THOU?
ᐒᐤ MOSES ᐟ

WHERE ARE YOU WHEN YOU'RE ASKED TO HELP SOMEONE IN NEED?

EXODUS 3:2–10 *There the angel of the Lord appeared to him in flames of fire from within a bush. Moses saw that though the bush was on fire it did not burn up. So Moses thought, "I will go over and see this strange sight—why the bush does not burn up."*

When the Lord saw that he had gone over to look, God called to him from within the bush, "Moses! Moses!" And Moses said, "Here I am."

"Do not come any closer," God said. "Take off your sandals, for the place where you are standing is holy ground." Then he said, "I am the God of your father, the God of Abraham, the God of Isaac and the God of Jacob." At this, Moses hid his face because he was afraid to look at God.

The Lord said, "I have indeed seen the misery of my people in Egypt. I have heard them crying out because of their slave drivers, and I am concerned about their suffering. So I have come down to rescue them from the hand of the Egyptians and bring them up out of that land into a good and spacious land, a land flowing with milk and honey—the home of the Canaanites, Hittites, Amorites, Perizzites, Hivites and Jebusites. And now the cry of the Israelites has reached me, and I have seen the way the Egyptians are oppressing them. So now, go. I am sending you to Pharaoh to bring my people the Israelites out of Egypt."

ᴄᴄᐟ WHERE ART THOU? ᐣᵒᵔ
MOSES

Where art thou, Moses?
He was hiding away
On the back of the desert,
Tending sheep every day.

But when it was time
For God's plan to resume,
God made a bush burn—
That fire didn't consume.

He made up excuses
Why he couldn't go:
"Please send someone else,
My speech is too slow."

Moses finally would listen
To what God had to say,
And followed the plan
Of God, day by day.

*W*HERE ART THOU?
⤳ DAVID ⤳

WHERE ARE YOU WHEN YOU'RE A MAN AFTER GOD'S HEART?

1 SAMUEL 17:45–51 *David said to the Philistine, "You come against me with sword and spear and javelin, but I come against you in the name of the Lord Almighty, the God of the armies of Israel, whom you have defied. This day the Lord will hand you over to me, and I'll strike you down and cut off your head. Today I will give the carcasses of the Philistine army to the birds of the air and the beasts of the earth, and the whole world will know that there is a God in Israel. All those gathered here will know that it is not by sword or spear that the Lord saves; but the battle is the Lord's and he will give all of you into our hands."*

⌖ WHERE ART THOU? ⌖
DAVID

Where art thou, David?
He was tending the sheep.
His devotion to God,
Every day he did keep.

The Israel army
All trembled with fear
As the threats of the Philistine
Every day they would hear.

Where art thou, David?
Goliath stands on the hill,
Who'll go fight this monster?
David answered, "I will."

We all know the story
Of David's success.
What God asked him to do,
David answered with "yes."

Every day of his life,
David made God a part,
We still know him today
As a man after God's heart.

*W*HERE ART THOU? JONAH

WHERE ARE YOU WHEN YOUR ATTITUDE NEEDS ADJUSTING?

JONAH 1:1–3 *The word of the Lord came to Jonah, son of Amittai: "Go to the great city of Nineveh and preach against it, because its wickedness has come up before me."*

But Jonah ran away from the Lord and headed for Tashish.

WHERE ART THOU? JONAH

Where art thou, Jonah?
I need you to go
To the city of Nineveh.
But Jonah said, "No."

He hopped on a ship—
A storm came with its fury.
The rebellion of Jonah
Became known in a hurry.

Three days in the fish
Doesn't seem very kind—
But that's what it took
To change Jonah's mind.

The fish spat him out
Upon the dry land,
Then Jonah was willing
To meet God's demand.

The people repented,
God spared the city,
Jonah was angry and pouted
And bathed in self pity.

WHERE ART THOU? SAUL (PAUL)

WHERE ARE YOU WHEN YOU THINK YOU ARE RIGHT, BUT ARE PROVEN WRONG?

ACTS 9:1–6 *Meanwhile, Saul was still breathing out murderous threats against the Lord's disciples. He went to the high priest and asked him for letters to the synagogues in Damascus, so that if he found any there who belonged to the Way, whether men or women, he might take them as prisoners to Jerusalem. As he neared Damascus on his journey, suddenly a light from heaven flashed around him. He fell to the ground and heard a voice say to him, "Saul, Saul, why do you persecute me?"*

"Who are you, Lord?" Saul asked. "I am Jesus, whom you are persecuting," he replied. "Now get up and go into the city, and you will be told what you must do."

WHERE ART THOU?
SAUL (PAUL)

Then there was Saul,
He thought he was right—
Killing the Christians
Each day and each night.

Where art thou, Saul?
As he fell to the ground,
A bright light from heaven
Flashed all around.

A life-changing experience
Saul had that day,
Those traveling with him
Had to lead him away.

Hearing from Jesus
Made Saul turn from his ways
And follow his Savior
The rest of his days.

WHERE ART THOU? REFRAIN

Now God has more ways
Than we could dare mention,
But he always knows how
To get our attention.

When God asks the question
Of just where we are—
To face up to the facts
Is much better by far.

All the sin in our life,
If we confess and believe
That Jesus is Lord,
Then forgiveness receive.

When God asks the question
If we are where we should be
We quickly can answer,
"Here am I—Lord, use me."

WHEN IS IT CHRISTMAS?

GOD'S GIFT TO MAN WAS GIVEN TO BE ENJOYED EVERY DAY OF THE YEAR

JOHN 3:16–17 *For God so loved the world that he gave his one and only Son that whoever believes in him shall not perish but have eternal life. For God did not send his Son into the world to condemn the world, but to save the world through him.*

December twenty-fifth has been chosen as the day that we celebrate the birth of Jesus. Exchanging gifts is a Christmas tradition enjoyed in many parts of the world. Much thought is put into shopping for the perfect gift for each person on the list. Once the gift is selected, wrapping paper, tape and ribbons are assembled and the gift is beautifully wrapped.

Then the gift is delivered and anticipation grows as the recipient unwraps the special package.

Reactions vary as the gift is revealed. Perhaps the gift is of such value that the receiver feels unworthy of accepting it. Pleasure may be expressed when receiving the gift, but then it is put away, forgotten about and never used. Some gifts are treasured and become more meaningful with daily use. Other gifts are immediately refused and returned to the giver.

God is the originator of gift giving. He loves us so much that he gave his very best gift, his son, Jesus Christ. The cry of a newborn baby announced Jesus' arrival on Earth. He was beautiful in Mary and Joseph's eyes, and he became the most cherished gift mankind would ever be given. This treasured gift is available to each one of us, but a decision must be made to either accept or reject what has been given to us. Do we feel unworthy? Christ's death on the cross for the forgiveness of our sins makes us worthy when we accept him. Do we only fellowship with Jesus when we're in a crisis, or do we treasure our time with him each day? Have we refused to accept the gift of Jesus?

When we accept Jesus Christ as our Savior, we celebrate "Christmas" every day of the year!

What does Christmas mean to you?

ᴄᴄ WHEN IS IT CHRISTMAS? ᴐᴐ

On February twenty-third
Nineteen hundred and fifty-one,
I received the gift
Of God's only son.

From that day forward
It was Christmas, you see,
Because Jesus was there
Walking with me.

A few short years later,
We became man and wife—
It was Christmas because
Christ was part of my life.

The time in the army
Were really tough years—
Again, Jesus was there
Even though there were tears.

As the children arrived,
How quickly they grew,
But Jesus was with us
All the way through.

Sometimes I would worry
About money and stuff,
But the Lord would remind me
There's always enough.

When the doctor advised me
"There's no more I can do,"
God's grace was sufficient
To carry us through.

The deaths in my family,
Several times I would face,
But Christ was there with me
Supplying the grace.

God gave us Jesus,
The world's greatest gift!
He's always here with us
To undergird and uplift.

It's Jesus here with us
Each moment each day,
As we walk, run or stumble
Upon life's pathway.

Is it Christmas today?
I hope you'll remember
That Christmas is more
Than the twenty-fifth of December!

PEACE, BE STILL

JESUS CALMS THE SEAS
AND WILL BE WITH US
THROUGH THE STORMS OF LIFE

MARK 4:35–41 *...on the same day, when evening had come, he said to them, "Let us cross over to the other side."*

Now when they had left the multitude, they took him along in the boat as he was. And other little boats were also with him.

And a great windstorm arose, and the waves beat into the boat, so that it was already filling, but he was in the stern, asleep on a pillow. And they awoke him and said to him. "Teacher, do you not care that we are perishing?"

Then he arose and rebuked the wind, and said to the sea, "Peace, be still": And the wind ceased and there was a great calm.

But he said to them, "Why are you so fearful? How is it that you have no faith?"

And they feared exceedingly, and said to one another, "Who can this be, that even the wind and the sea obey him!"

The majestic, towering clouds of a huge thunderstorm—the dazzling display of lightning zigzagging across the sky—the vibrating boom of thunder is quite an exhilarating thing to behold. That is, if the storm is being viewed from a distance. To be in the middle of the storm and exposed to the danger of it is a completely different scenario.

In the Gospel of Mark 4:35–41, we read the story of a powerful storm on the Sea of Galilee. The sea was calm when Jesus and his disciples set out in a boat to sail to the other shore. Jesus was tired from ministering throughout the day to the large crowds of people that had gathered, and the Scriptures tell us that he curled up on a cushion and fell asleep. Partway through the trip, a furious squall suddenly developed and strong winds and high waves threatened to swamp the boat. The disciples feared for their lives and, in a panic, woke Jesus up, begging him to help them. Jesus wasn't frightened by the storm and as he spoke the words, "Peace, be still," the wind and waves instantly ceased.

Storms may come into our lives as suddenly and unexpectedly as the storm hit on the Sea of Galilee. We may face illness, loss of employment and financial problems, the end of a marriage, or death of loved ones. There may be times when it seems as though the storm is so huge that it will last forever and that we might not survive. Those are the times when we cling a little tighter to the Savior and ask him to quiet the storm that rages around us.

Philippians 4:7 assures us, "And the peace of God, which transcends all understanding, will guard your hearts and your minds in Christ Jesus." The Lord is able to calm the storm that threatens to swamp you.

Will you listen for his voice as he whispers,
"Peace, be still"?

⌒ PEACE, BE STILL ⌒

Is Jesus in your boat today?
Is he on the shore or far away?
Is he a daily part of life?
Or only called when there's great strife?

Things may be going great today,
But tomorrow's skies may turn to gray,
Life can so quickly take a turn
And big black clouds around us churn.

You may be young and far from home,
For the first time knowing you're all alone.
Jesus is knocking at your heart's door,
Saying, "I'll be with you evermore";

Or a single parent trying to make ends meet,
The kids need shoes for their growing feet.
There's not enough money to go around,
You wonder if things will ever settle down.

Your spouse is grouchy and picks a fight,
Or never comes home 'til late at night.
You know there's alcohol or drug abuse,
And you often think, "What's the use?"

When sickness comes and lies at our door
And the doctors say they can do no more—
Lord, we give this one to you,
But we need your peace to see us through!

Perhaps your best friend has let you down,
Or your trusted spouse is running around;
Your little ones need so much care,
And your teenage child has a rebellious flare!

Your aged parent can't stay alone,
It's time to look for a nursing home.
Everyone around you demands your time,
Or you just can't keep things all in line.

You're called in to work, and you aren't ready,
But you're the one who must keep things steady;
The demands on you seem to increase—
With all these things, Lord, we need your peace!

When death suddenly comes to your home,
And you find yourself now all alone,
You ask for peace to come your way,
So you can make it through the day.

Suddenly, you're tossed all around,
Can't get your feet on solid ground,
It's time to stop and call his name,
Remind yourself he's still the same.

You do not know what will come your way
As your life goes on from day to day.
Lord, let us know we are in your will
And hear your voice say, "Peace, Be Still."

Our confidence must be in you
To know each day you'll see us through,
The storms of life will never cease,
But we can make it with your peace.

Do you have peace in the dark of night?
That will see you through 'til the morning light?
Is Jesus in your boat today?
Is he on the shore or far away?

$\mathcal{A}$ Recipe for Happiness

Giving is more than a few dollars in the offering

Luke 6:32–38 *If you love those who love you, what credit is that to you? Even sinners love those who love them. And if you do good to those who are good to you what credit is that to you? Even sinners do that. And if you lend to those from whom you expect repayment, what credit is that to you? Even "sinners" lend to "sinners" expecting to be repaid in full.*

But love your enemies, do good to them, and lend to them without expecting to get anything back. Then your reward will be great, and you will be sons of the Most High, because he is kind to the ungrateful and wicked. Be merciful, just as your Father is merciful.

Do not judge and you will not be judged. Do not condemn, and you will not be condemned. Forgive, and you will be forgiven. Give, and it will be given to you. A good measure pressed down, shaken together and running over, will be poured into your lap. For with the measure you use, it will be measured to you.

A newborn baby is totally helpless and can do nothing to take care of itself. It starts its life being served by everyone around it. As the child grows older, parents do their best to change that pattern. When my granddaughter, Revonna, was just a toddler, I stopped by to give her a small toy that I had purchased for her. Within a few minutes, she disappeared to her room and returned with a pink, stuffed dinosaur that she loved and handed to me. I was about ready to give it back to her when her Daddy said, "No, Mom, you need to accept the dinosaur, she needs to learn how to give as well as to receive." Revonna and I both enjoyed the joy of giving that day.

Luke 6:38 is often quoted in regard to finances; it's good to remember that serving others is also giving. In Matthew 25, Jesus told us that whatever we do to serve others is actually serving him!

We have been involved in the healthcare field, caring for the elderly for many years. There are many opportunities to serve in this field. A quick hug for a lonely grandma warms her heart, and a pat on the knee and a shared laugh makes a grandpa's day. There is immense satisfaction in helping someone eat a meal when they are no longer able to feed themselves. It takes so little to serve someone less fortunate than we are, yet we receive so much joy in return.

*Have you experienced the joy and happiness
that serving others brings?*

A RECIPE FOR HAPPINESS

Happiness is that something
We create in our mind,
Not something that we search for
Just hoping that we find.

It's just waking up—each morning
At the beginning of the day—
Counting all our blessings
And remembering to pray.

It's giving up the thoughts
That breed strife and discontent,
And accepting what comes our way
As gifts from heaven sent.

It's giving up the wishing for
The things that we have not;
It's being always thankful for
The little things we've got.

It's knowing that each breath we take
Is a gift from God above;
It's in the joy of serving others
That we really learn God's love.

It's in looking for the many things
God gives us every day,
Then sharing them with others
That we meet along life's way.

It's by doing all the little things
God gives us opportunity to do,
That we find real contentment
And genuine happiness, too.

$\mathcal{G}$od's Handfuls on Purpose

Beautiful story of Ruth's love and devotion

Ruth 2:2–17 *And Ruth the Moabitess said to Naomi, "Let me go to the fields and pick up the leftover grain behind any in whose eyes I find favor." Naomi said to her, "Go ahead my daughter," so she went out and began to glean in the fields behind the harvesters. As it turned out, she found herself working in a field belonging to Boaz who was from the clan of Elimelech.*

Just then Boaz arrived from Bethlehem and greeted the harvesters, "The Lord be with you!" "The Lord Bless you!" they called back.

Boaz asked the foreman of his harvesters, "Whose young woman is that?"

The foreman replied, "She is the Moabitess who came back from Moab with Naomi. She said, 'Please let me glean and gather among the sheaves behind the harvesters.' She went into the field and has worked steadily from morning 'til now, except for a short rest in the shelter."

So Boaz said to Ruth, "My daughter, listen to me, don't go and glean in another field and don't go away from here. Stay here with my servant girls. Watch the field where the men are harvesting, and follow along after the girls. I have told the men not to touch you. And whenever you are thirsty, go and get a drink from the water jars the men have filled."

At this, she bowed down with her face to the ground. She exclaimed, "Why have I found such favor in your eyes that you notice me— a foreigner?"

Boaz replied, "I've been told all about what you have done for your mother-in-law since the death of your husband—how you left your father and mother and your homeland and came to live with a people you did not know before. May the Lord repay you for what you have done. May you be richly rewarded by the Lord God of Israel, under whose wings you have come to take refuge."

"May I continue to find favor in your eyes, my Lord," she said, "You have given *me comfort and have spoken kindly to your servant—though I do not have the standing of one of your servant girls."*

At mealtime Boaz said to her, "Come over here. Have some bread and dip it in the wine vinegar."

When she sat down with the harvesters, he offered her some roasted grain. She ate all she wanted and had some left over. As she got up to glean, Boaz gave orders to his men, "Even if she gathers among the sheaves, don't embarrass her. Rather pull out some stalks for her from the bundles and leave them for her to pick up. And don't rebuke her."

The Book of Ruth begins with a famine in the land and ends with the birth of a baby who would have a place in the lineage of Christ. Elimelech, Naomi and their two sons left Bethlehem and moved to the land of Moab to escape the severe famine that had struck the land of Judah. The sons married Orpha and Ruth who were from Moab.

As time went on, Naomi's husband and both of her sons died and the women made a decision to return to Bethlehem. However, when it came time to leave, Orpha returned to her own family. Ruth chose to stay with Naomi, declaring her devotion to her as well as to her God. Naomi and Ruth made the hard journey back to Judah and arrived with only what they could carry.

It was the law that during harvest time the corners of the fields were to be left unharvested so that the poor could gather grain. It was necessary for Ruth to provide food and she went to the fields to gather bits of grain. Boaz, the wealthy owner of the field and a close relative of Naomi, recognized Ruth and spoke to her. In appreciation for the loving and kind way that she treated Naomi, he instructed the reapers in his field to purposely leave handfuls of grain behind so that it would be easier for Ruth to gather the grain. He also invited her to eat meals with the workers in his fields. As the story continues, we read that Boaz and Ruth married, and a son, Obed, was born to them. Obed became the grandfather of David and part of the genealogy of Christ.

Because of Ruth's faithfulness to God and to Naomi, God rewarded her with *handfuls of blessings*. Extra barley was easily available to be harvested and provided for immediate physical needs. She found favor with Boaz who became her protector and later her husband. He was a generous man and provided a secure home for Ruth and Naomi. God gave Boaz and Ruth a son to carry on the family name. God's *handfuls on purpose* completely changed Ruth's life.

God continues to provide *handfuls of blessings on purpose* to his people. His blessings are around us each day in every-day happenings that we often take for granted. Some blessings provide comfort or meet needs; others determine the *big* things in life. It's a blessing to be born in America and have the opportunity to obtain a good education and a career. Being able to raise a family in a safe, healthy environment is another blessing. Knowing Jesus as Savior and Lord is a priceless blessing.

Do you recognize God's
handfuls on purpose *in your life?*

GOD'S HANDFULS
ON PURPOSE

God's *handfuls on purpose*
Are there every day;
Do we find ourselves thankful
When they come our way?

We've all found ourselves
In a full parking lot,
When suddenly before us
Is a nice parking spot.

We're balancing our checkbook
And the numbers don't add,
When right there is the answer—
Oh boy are we glad!

Or we're moping around
And nothing seems right,
When right there is the person
Who is cheerful and bright.

Our family is in need
And we don't have a dime;
When the job offer comes
At just the right time.

The car's broken down
Parked on the road side,
Along comes a stranger,
And gives us a ride.

We're sick as can be—
Outside it is winter—
Our family is hungry
And a neighbor brings dinner.

We've had some bad luck—
Our leg's in a cast—
In stops a friend,
Says he'll cut the grass.

Maybe we'll say those are
Just things that friends do—
But always remember that God
Gives us friends, too.

For the *handfuls on purpose*
That are scattered our way;
Do we take them for granted?
Do we thank God each day?

Do you know the joy
Of helping others in need?
Or do we bathe in self-pity,
Wrapped up in our greed?

Do we find ourselves willing
Handfuls on purpose to give?
Or do we selfishly keep them,
Which way do we live?

Lord, help us remember
Good things come from you—
To share them with others
Is what you'd have us do.

WHAT HAVE YOU DONE WITH THE GIFT?

HAS THE BABY IN THE MANGER BECOME LORD OF YOUR LIFE?

JOHN 3:16 (KJV) *For God so loved the world that he gave his only begotten son, that whoever believes in him should not perish but have everlasting life.*

Shopping for just the right gift, wrapping it with beautiful paper, finishing it off with a perfectly tied bow and presenting it to that special person is great fun! Some gifts are practical and useful, some gifts add to a prized collection, other gifts might have special meaning. It really doesn't matter what the gift is or the packaging that it comes in. What matters the most is that it is given in love.

Jesus, God's gift to us, didn't come to earth wearing a jeweled crown and royal robes. He didn't come to earth to sit on an elaborate, gold throne. He came to earth as a newborn baby, wrapped in plain cloth and placed in a stable manger. He was not readily accepted by everyone. King Herod sought to kill him when he heard of his birth. Some religious leaders tried to discredit his teaching and often he was mocked.

God's gift of his only son, Jesus, is priceless. It can not be purchased. It is free to all who will accept Jesus as Savior and believe in him.

What will you do with your gift?

WHAT HAVE YOU DONE WITH THE GIFT?

What have I done
With gifts given to me—
That were planned in advance
As to just what they should be?

They were bought with great care,
Planned especially for me—
Wrapped up in a package
Placed under the tree.

The gifts—they were varied,
Some useful, some fun—
I opened them carefully
And thanked everyone.

What if just this one gift
Was just set aside—
'Cause the wrapping was plain
And how it was tied?

If you'd sent that gift
And love was your reason,
It wasn't even acknowledged,
Not part of the season.

How would you feel
If you were this one,
And the gift that you'd sent
Had cost you your son?

Or if you were the son,
Suffering pain and disgrace,
Mocking, scoffing and jeering,
And spit in your face?

The gift that was sent,
We could never afford;
The best heaven had,
It was Jesus our Lord.

Now, how can a gift
Be so priceless yet free,
But given only to those
Who receive it, you see.

Now we all have the choice
If this gift we receive—
But to really possess it,
We have to believe.

He'll come into your life,
Your Savior he'll be,
God's most priceless gift,
Yet to us it is free.

He'll always be with us
As a friend and a brother,
A life-long companion,
He's there like no other.

He'll be all that you need,
He'll sustain and uplift—
My question to you:
What have you done with God's gift?

$\mathscr{I}$ DON'T UNDERSTAND
(JOHN 3:16)

HAS JOHN 3:16 BECOME A PART OF YOUR PERSONAL LIFE?

JOHN 3:16 **(KJV)** *For God so loved the world that he gave his only begotten Son, that whoever believes in him should not perish but have everlasting life.*

$\mathscr{I}$t was a very cold night when someone told a little homeless boy to knock on the door of the big, white house. He was told that when the owners of the house came to the door he should say, "John 3:16," and he would be let into the house. He knocked on the door and soon found himself sitting by a warm fire. He thought to himself, *John 3:16; I don't understand, but sure makes a cold boy warm.*

A hot, filling meal was provided for him to eat and as he ate he thought, *John 3:16; I don't understand, but sure makes a hungry boy feel full.*

A nice warm bath was drawn for him and as he soaked in the bathtub he thought, *John 3:16; I don't understand, but sure makes a dirty boy feel clean.*

Later, as he was tucked into a warm, comfy bed, he thought, *John 3:16; I don't understand, but sure makes a tired boy feel rested.*

The next morning during devotions the lady of the house read John 3:16 to him from the Bible and he thought, *John 3:16; I don't understand, but sure makes a lost boy feel safe.*

It may be hard for us to comprehend the depth of God's love that he would send his only son, Jesus, to earth just for us, but he did. It may be hard for us to understand why Jesus would be born as a baby, experience the hardships of life, be crucified on a cross, be buried and rise again after three days to redeem us from our sins, but he was.

God's love has no boundaries. I don't fully understand, but I know that it is true.

Does John 3:16 have real meaning for you?

I DON'T UNDERSTAND
(JOHN 3:16)

I don't understand
God's magnificent love—
As he stood in heaven
And looked down from above.

I don't understand
Why Jesus would come—
When heaven was home
And he was God's only son.

I don't understand
Why Jesus must die—
How the blood that he shed
Could save you and I.

I don't understand
Why this gift I receive—
Eternal life—is all mine
If I only believe.

I don't understand
How from sin I am free—
When the sin was all mine,
But Jesus paid it for me.

No, I don't understand
God's wonderful plan—
It's simply a miracle
That God gives to man.

The plan is so simple
I've tried it—it's true—
What does John 3:16
Really mean to you?

Choices
(The Power of Choice)

Adam and Eve, Noah, Abram, Lot, Ruth—their choices and the consequences

Genesis 3:6–7 *When the woman saw that the fruit of the tree was good for food and pleasing to the eye, and also desirable for gaining wisdom, she took some and ate it. She also gave some to her husband, who was with her, and he ate it. Then the eyes of both of them were opened and they realized they were naked: so they sewed fig leaves together and made coverings for themselves.*

Genesis 7:1–4 *The Lord then said to Noah, "Go into the ark, you and your whole family, because I have found you righteous in this generation. Take with you seven of every kind of clean animal, a male and its mate, and two* of every kind of unclean animal, a male and its mate, and also seven of every kind of bird, male and female, to keep their various kinds alive throughout the earth. Seven days from now I will send rain on the earth for forty days and forty nights, and I will wipe from the face of the earth every living creature I have made."

GENESIS 13:8–12 So Abram said to Lot, "Let's not have any quarreling between you and me, or between your herdsmen and mine, for we are brothers. Is not the whole land before you? Let's part company. If you go to the left, I'll go to right; if you go to the right, I'll go to the left."

Lot looked up and saw that the whole plain of the Jordan was well watered like the garden of the Lord, like the land of Egypt, toward Zoar, (This was before the Lord destroyed Sodom and Gomorrah.) So Lot chose for himself the whole plain of the Jordan and set out toward the east. The two men parted company; Abram lived in the land of Canaan, while Lot lived among the cities of the plain and pitched his tents near Sodom.

GENESIS 13:18 So Abram moved his tents and went to live near the great trees of Mamre at Hebron, where he built an altar to the Lord.

Ruth 1:16 *But Ruth replied, "Don't urge me to leave you or to turn back from you. Where you go I will go, and where you stay I will stay. Your people will be my people and your God my God."*

Life changing choices that made a difference in many peoples' lives

God made man with the power of choice, and the Bible gives us examples of men and women who made bad choices and good choices.

*L*ot and Abram (God later changed Abram's name to Abraham) raised their flocks and became quite prosperous. The time came for them to part company, and Lot chose the most fertile of the land. Soon, life in the city enticed him, and he made the bad choice to move his family into a city whose inhabitants lived very wicked lifestyles. God became very angry with the wickedness of the city and vowed to destroy it, but Abram bargained with God to save his nephew, Lot, and his family. God honored Abram's request and allowed Lot, his wife and his two daughters to flee the city. They were instructed not to look back, but Lot's wife chose to disobey and was turned into a pillar of salt. Because of the choices that Lot made, his life was radically changed. He and his two daughters lost all of their material possessions and ended up living in a cave.

Abram and Sarah had one great sadness in their lives. Sarah was barren and they desperately wanted a son. God made a covenant with Abram and promised that he would have a son and that he should name him Isaac. Abram chose to believe God even though it didn't seem possible for Sarah to have a child. God was true to his word. Abram was one-hundred years old and Sarah was ninety when Isaac was born to them. A few years later God instructed Abram to take his beloved son, Isaac, to the mountains in the region of Moriah and sacrifice him. Abram chose to trust God and obey his instructions and because of his choice, God provided an alternate substitute to sacrifice and spared Isaac's life.

The choices that we make determine who we will become. The choices that young people make to obey their parents; and the friends that they choose help to shape their character. We continue to make choices as we progress through life—making career choices and perhaps choosing a spouse. We make countless choices throughout the day such as controlling our attitudes when things don't always go as anticipated and living our lives with integrity.

The most important choice that we will make in our lifetime is the choice to believe in Jesus; study his word; trust in him and accept him as our Savior.

Have you made that choice?

ᏋᏋ CHOICES ᏩᏩ
(THE POWER OF CHOICE)

We all make choices every day—
Where we go and what we say,
What we eat, how much we drink,
How we act and what we think.

Where we work and how we play—
We set our priorities every day.
How we think and how we live,
What we take and what we give.

The choices start when we're very young,
We must control our naughty tongue.
As we make choices one by one,
They will decide who we become.

To tell the whole truth or to simply lie—
A choice we'll make 'til the day we die.
The friends we choose show who we are—
Will they serve us well or leave a scar?

The choice of profession, which way should we go,
For some it's confusing and others just know.
How will the days of our lives be spent?
Can we make a living and remain content?

Then there are the choices that sculpt our life,
Like the one that we choose for a husband or wife.
The choice to have children will change how we live—
How quickly we learn of ourselves we must give.

The way that we act, and the words that we say
Will make a big difference in lives every day.
Our attitude shows, but it's always our choice,
It will also reflect in the tone of our voice.

The choice is all mine to be grouchy or sweet
And will be quickly detected by the people we meet.
What do our friends see as we come in for the day?
Do they greet us with pleasure or stay out of our way?

We can blame the bad coffee or maybe our spouse,
Or the fact that the kids made a mess of the house.
The traffic was slow or our car wouldn't start—
Still, our mood for today is a choice on our part.

Do we really believe that the Bible is true?
Or do we just go to church to fill up a pew?
When the Bible says "sinner" does it really mean me?
Does it take Jesus' blood before I am free?

Do I truly believe Jesus died on the cross
To pay for my sins because I was lost?
That his blood will cover the bad things that I've done?
That my sins are all gone because of God's son?

Do I read his word daily? That's really my choice.
Do I prayerfully listen to hear his sweet voice?
Has his love really changed me; the things that I do?
Do the people around me see Jesus come through?

When reading his word do I hear his sweet voice?
And believe that he made me a creature of choice?
We can blame who we want but make no mistake
Our life's a result of the choices we make!

The Joy of Giving

Giving comes in many forms, each of us has something different to give

Acts 20:33–35 *I have not coveted anyone's silver or gold or clothing. You yourselves know that these hands of mine have supplied my own needs and the needs of my companions. In everything I did, I showed you that by this kind of hard work we must help the weak, remembering the words the Lord Jesus himself said: "It is more blessed to give than to receive."*

Luke 6:38 *Give, and it will be given to you. A good measure, pressed down, shaken together and running over, will be poured into your lap. For with the measure you use, it will be measured to you.*

1 Peter 4:9–11 *Offer hospitality to one another without grumbling. Each one should* *use whatever gift he has received to serve others, faithfully administering God's grace in its various forms. If anyone speaks, he should do it as one speaking the very words of God. If anyone serves, he should do it with the strength God provides, so that in all things God may be praised through Jesus Christ. Amen.*

2 CORINTHIANS 9:7 Each man should give what he has decided in his heart to give, not reluctantly or under compulsion, for God loves a cheerful giver.

*O*ur society would lead us to believe the opposite of that scripture. Statistics show that 80 percent of us are "takers" and only 20 percent of us are "givers." Perhaps we don't practice giving because we associate giving in a monetary sense and we don't have the means to give. There are many ways to give that don't include money. Have you ever experienced the great joy and satisfaction of being a good friend offering a listening ear and helping to make a life easier? Have you ever folded your arms around someone who is grieving and comforted them with your love? Have you ever seen the smile on a troubled teenager's face when you offered a word of encouragement or praise? Have you ever put your own schedule on hold to give the gift of time as a volunteer at a nursing home, offered to drive an elderly person to an appointment, or rocked a child who needs reassurance? If your answer is yes to any of these questions, you are a giver of yourself.

Sometimes gifts are given out of a sense of duty or with the idea that something will be given in return. God is our example of a true giver. He gave his son to die for all mankind, knowing that many would never acknowledge or accept his gift. He showed his great love when he gave his greatest treasure, his only son, Jesus.

Will you accept his gift?

∽ THE JOY OF GIVING ∽

Have we found the treasure
In our day-to-day living,
From a heart full of love
And the great joy in giving.

Our chances to give
Are endless each day—
To make someone's life better,
Or are we there just for the pay?

We may not have money
To give lavish gifts,
So give of yourself—
Be a friend that uplifts.

Have you felt the great joy
To give a child her first doll?
Or in helping a brother
From a self-imposed fall?

For the teen who is struggling
To become an adult—
Do we uplift and encourage
Or just always find fault?

Are we quick to give praise
Every day as we should,
When encouragement is needed
Do we make people feel good?

The Bible speaks clearly
Of sowing good seed,
And helping each other
When we see a need.

Do we give of our dollars
To help with a great loss?
If we all give a portion,
We can help cover the cost.

We can give of ourselves—
Maybe just lend an ear
To that someone who's lonely
And has no family near.

The greatest pleasure in life
Is not just to succeed,
It's the satisfaction and joy
Of helping someone in need.

We've missed a great deal
Of the pleasure of living
If we haven't experienced
The great joy of giving.

God gave us his son
With love from his heart,
The great plan of salvation
so we can all have a part.

What will we take with us
When we leave this earth?
The same we came in with
At the time of our birth.

What really will count
When we get to heaven?
Not what we've received,
Only what we have given.

$\mathcal{E}$NOUGH
(The Refiner of Silver)

How the Lord
is the Refiner of our Lives

Malachi 3:2–4 *But who can endure the day of his coming? Who can stand when he appears? For he will be like a refiner's fire or a launderer's soap. He will sit as a refiner and purifier of silver; he will purify the Levites and refine them like gold and silver. Then the Lord will have men who will bring offerings in righteousness and the offerings of Judah and Jerusalem will be acceptable to the Lord, as in days gone by; as in former years.*

The story is told about a group of ladies involved in a Bible study who were discussing the scripture found in Malachi 3:3 "He will sit as a refiner and purifier of silver..." They wondered how this scripture applied to the character and nature of God. One of the women offered to find out about the process of refining silver and report her findings at the next Bible study.

That week she made a call to a silversmith and made an appointment to watch him at work. She didn't mention anything about the reason for her interest beyond her curiosity about the process of refining silver.

She watched as the silversmith held the silver compound over the fire. He explained that it needed to be held in the middle of the fire where the flames were the hottest so that all the impurities would be burned away. He went on to explain that he needed to stay in front of the fire the whole time to carefully watch the refining process because if the silver was left a moment too long in the flames, it would be destroyed.

The woman thought about the times that she had faced some "hot spots" in her life and how God had been right there with her through the "firestorms" in her life. She was silent for a moment and then asked the silversmith, "How do you know when the silver is fully refined?"

He smiled at her and answered, "Oh, that's easy, I know it's refined when I can see my image in it."

There's nothing pretty or useful about the ore that silver is found in. The silver product that we see used in beautiful, durable products emerges only after several processes and intense heat is applied during the refining stage.

Jesus Christ is the refiner of our lives that are full of impurities just as the chunks of ore are. Jesus looks past those impurities and sees the silver within. As we study scripture to learn more about him, we learn to trust our refiner, our Savior, who paid the price for our sins with his death on Calvary's cross. We have the assurance that he works within us; refining our lives so that his image will be seen in us.

Will you allow Jesus to refine your life?

ꭓꭓ ENOUGH ꭓꭓ
(THE REFINER OF SILVER)

Will I be silver…maybe bronze…maybe gold?
As day after day my life will unfold.

Have I had enough sunshine to brighten my days?
Have I had enough sorrows to soften my ways?

Have I had enough freedom to make my own choice?
Have I had enough correction to hear conscience voice?

Have I had the good fortune to know a strong body is wealth?
Have I had enough sickness to treasure my health?

Have I had enough loss so my life is never the same—
To treasure and love the ones that remain.

Do I give enough time to my family each day
So my commitment stays strong and my heart doesn't stray?

Am I ready and willing to go through the fire?
To give up my dreams and my selfish desire?

Do I trust him completely as the heat is applied?
Knowing each moment he'll be right by my side.

Will I do what is right when the fire gets hot?
Will I trust the refiner and remain in his pot?

We all make the choice at the end of the day
To let him refine us or go our own way.

We just have to remember when the going gets tough
That the refiner will know when we've had just enough.

Has enough of Jesus' blood to my heart been applied?
Do I remind myself daily for my sins Jesus died?

Have I had enough teaching to know the Bible is true?
Spent enough time with the Lord so his image shines through?

Has enough of God's word been hidden in my heart
So the desire is gone and sin has no part?

Has enough heat been applied to burn out the dross?
Am I willing to walk in the way of the cross?

How long will it take 'til from this fire I am free?
When I stand in judgment will God see Jesus in me?

THE PRODIGAL SON
ᶜᵉᶜ PART 1 ᵒᵒ
WHAT ARE YOU LOOKING FOR?

THE LOST SHEEP, THE LOST COIN,
THE LOST SON, OR SOMETHING ELSE?
EVERYONE IS LOOKING FOR SOMETHING.

LUKE 15:3–5 *Then Jesus told them this parable: "Suppose one of you has a hundred sheep and loses one of them. Does he not leave the ninety-nine in the open country and go after the lost sheep until he finds it? And when he finds it, he joyfully puts it on his shoulders and goes home."*

LUKE 15:8 *"Or suppose a woman has ten silver coins and loses one. Does she not light a lamp, sweep the house and search carefully until she finds it?"*

LUKE 15: 11–24 *Jesus continued: "There was a man who had two sons. The younger one said to his father, 'Father, give me my share of the estate.' So he divided his property between them. Not long after that, the younger son got together all he had, set off for a distant country and there squandered his wealth in wild living. After he had spent everything, there was a severe famine in that whole country, and he began to be in need. So he went and hired himself out to a citizen of that country, who sent him to his fields to feed pigs. He longed to fill his stomach with the pods that the pigs were eating, but no one gave him anything."*

"When he came to his senses, he said, 'How many of my father's hired men have food to spare, and here I am starving to death! I will set out and go back to my father and say to him: Father, I have sinned against heaven and against you. I am no longer worthy to be called your son; make me like one of your hired men.' So he got up and went to his father."

"But while he was still a long way off, his father saw him and was filled with compassion for him; he ran to his son, threw his arms around him and kissed him."

"The son said to him, 'Father, I have sinned against heaven and against you. I am no longer worthy to be called your son.'"

"But the father said to his servants, 'Quick! Bring the best robe and put it on him. Put a ring on his finger and sandals on his feet. Bring the fattened calf and kill it. Let's have a feast and celebrate. For this son of mine was dead and is alive again; he was lost and is found.' So they began to celebrate."

*I*f you have ever lost something that you value, you probably can still recall that feeling in the pit of your stomach of great loss. Chapter 15 of Luke records three parables about loss that Jesus taught.

The shepherd gathered his flock together and discovered that there were only ninety-nine sheep...one was missing. He desperately searched until he found the one lost sheep and rejoiced when the flock was complete once again.

A woman had ten valuable silver coins, but one day she discovered that one of them was missing. She diligently searched her house until the lost treasure was found, and then she called her friends and neighbors to rejoice with her.

A man had two sons. The older son stayed home and worked with his father. The younger son was eager to experience and explore what the world had to offer. He took his share of the estate and left home. He squandered away his money; his friends deserted him; and he ended up destitute. One day he realized how foolish he had been and began to make his way back home. His father had been longingly looking for him to return, and one day he saw him walking toward home. He ran to his son and welcomed him with total acceptance—rejoicing that his son had returned to the family.

God, our Father, does the same for us. When we take the first step toward him in repentance, he accepts us just as we are. He's not interested in our past, only our future with him. You may be like the one lost sheep who has wandered away from the shepherd. Or perhaps your life resembles the lost coin, only living for treasure or material wealth. Maybe you've chosen the path of the prodigal son and have hit rock bottom with your life. God stands with outstretched arms and rejoices as he welcomes you into his family.

"For God so loved the world that he gave his one and only Son, that whoever believes in him shall not perish but have eternal life." John 3:16 (NIV)

God is watching and waiting for you.
Will you come to him now?

THE PRODIGAL SON
PART 1
WHAT ARE YOU LOOKING FOR?

We're all looking for something as we travel life's way.
As we get up each morning and face a new day.

When we're young, it's adventure…to explore this big world.
From morning 'til evening, in our beds we are curled.

Then school's the new place where we look for new friends
And we're constantly looking…'til the last school year ends.

We look for new clothes…they must all be just right
With the hottest brand name…sloppy and loose…or skin tight.

Then comes the years when our hearts are in whirls,
Girls are looking for guys…and guys are looking for girls.

There are houses and cars, and travel and stuff,
We're not satisfied, we don't have quite enough.

We will all make the choice…which pathway we trod.
Often it's all about "me"… never thinking of God.

We may be the "lamb" who is starting to stray
But responds to the shepherd as he corrects us each day.

We may be the "lost coin"…looking only for treasure.
Living only for wealth to see how much we can measure?

Or we may be the "son" who has gone his own way,
Who finds himself destitute at the end of the day?

When I come to my senses…what will I see?
Will I think of "the Father" who is waiting for me?

Will I truly repent…admit I have sinned?
In hopes that my Father will take me back in.

I have nothing to offer but my guilt and my shame
I'm no longer worthy…to call my Father by name.

He will welcome me back…not as servant, but as son
He's been watching and waiting, he's so glad that I've come.

Because he is God…he'll forgive all my sin,
He'll welcome me home, and bring me back in.

He'll clean up the filth…that I've wallowed in.
Because of his nature…he'll forget where I've been.

Joint heirs with Jesus is what we receive
If we come to God…repent and believe.

The Father is watching and waiting for us to come home.
Will we return to him now…or stay away and alone?

THE PRODIGAL SON
‿ PART 2 ‿
THE BROTHER

THE "LOST SON" RETURNS AND "THE BROTHER" HAS AN ATTITUDE!

[Jesus continued with the parable]
LUKE 15:25–32 *"Meanwhile, the older son was in the field. When he came near the house, he heard music and dancing. So he called one of the servants and asked him what was going on. 'Your brother has come,' he replied, 'and your father has killed the fattened calf because he has him back safe and sound.'"*

"The older brother became angry and refused to go in. So his father went out and pleaded with him. But he answered his father, 'Look! All these years I've been slaving for you and never disobeyed your orders. Yet you never gave me even a young goat so I could

celebrate with my friends. But when this son of yours who has squandered your property with prostitutes comes home, you kill the fattened calf for him!'"

"'My son,' the father said, 'you are always with me, and everything I have is yours. But we had to celebrate and be glad, because this brother of yours was dead and is alive again; he was lost and is found.'"

There are many family dynamics in the parable of the prodigal son found in the fifteenth chapter of the Gospel of Luke. The father in this story never gave up on his son and anxiously watched and waited for his return. He rejoiced and showed great compassion when his son did return home.

The rebellious son returned broken and destitute. The fabulous life that he had anticipated had turned out to be just the opposite for him. He returned with a contrite heart and begged for forgiveness and the opportunity to come home as a servant, or become part of the family again.

His brother who had remained obedient to his father and had worked hard through the years was very jealous and felt neglected and unappreciated. He resented the big celebration prepared for his wayward brother.

The father of the two young men commended his son for working faithfully throughout the years. He encouraged his son to accept the disgraced brother and to celebrate his return home to the family.

This parable is a wonderful example for us and how we relate to others. Do we turn our backs on someone who isn't exactly like us? When we see someone suffering, do we consider them someone else's problem? Or do we celebrate when someone has repented of a destructive lifestyle and asks for a second chance?

God does! Each person is valuable to him. He never gives up on us no matter how far we have strayed from him. He welcomes us back to his family with open arms when we repent and ask for his forgiveness.

Do you know someone who needs your
forgiveness and help to restore their life?

THE PRODIGAL SON PART 2: THE BROTHER

Now I am the brother, who stayed home with you, Dad.
When he left with his fortune…and you were so sad.

All these years I have worked…tried to be a good son,
When help or comfort you needed…I was the one.

Up early each morning…worked all through the day,
No parties with friends…and no time to play.

My brother's been gone for a good many years,
Not seeing your pain…or you shedding tears.

He did things that were wrong…although he knew better,
Never a thought of you, Father…not even a letter.

He only thought of himself…just have a good time,
Didn't care that he squandered your very last dime.

He was ragged and dirty…smelled like the pig pen,
You hugged him and kissed him…and brought him right in.

You put on a clean robe and a ring that is new,
Now you ask me to rejoice with you, too?

The father's reply was gentle in part,
But the words that he spoke came straight from his heart.

You've been a good son…I'm so glad I've had you,
All my possessions belong to you, too.

Our family's been broken…so great was the cost,
Your brother's been missing…I've had a son that was lost!

Your brother was lost…and now he is found,
Can't you rejoice and be glad, let the music resound?

We all need forgiveness, the lost sheep and the son,
Thank God for a Savior who forgives us each one.

Do we find it hard…When a new Christian comes in…
To accept him as "brother"and forget where he's been?

God simply reminds us…that he is our brother,
He was lost, has come home…we must forgive all the other.

Can we forget his transgressions and help him recover?
Can we rejoice with the Father…and accept him as brother?

Let's rejoice and be glad…we're no longer alone.
Our brother was lost…at last he is home.

FAMILY & FRIENDS

The Arent Family
back row: *Elaine, Leslie, Bob, Howard, Eldora;*
front row: *Lyle, Effie, Herman, and Alvin, 1953*

'Hayfield Lunch'
Bob, Eldora, Effie, Herman, Lyle, and Alvin.
circa 1950

Herman Arent
and Effie Jones.
circa 1923

Arent family—
back row: Effie, Herman, Howard;
front row: Bob, Eldora, Leslie,
and Elaine. circa 1940

Herman and Effie Jones, 1964

Arent family—Baby Lyle, Herman, Bob,
Elaine, Eldora, Effie, and Alvin. circa 1945
(Howard and Leslie were serving overseas in World War II)

THANK GOD FOR MY CHILDHOOD

BEING A WISE STEWARD

> **PROVERBS 1:7–9** *(TLBP) How does a man become wise? The first step is to trust and reverence the Lord! Only fools refuse to be taught. Listen to your father and mother. What you learn from them will stand you in good stead; it will gain you many honors.*

I'm thankful for the stewardship example that my parents set before us. They worked hard to provide a good life for their seven children. My dad spent long hours working in the fields and taking care of the livestock. My mother was an expert at putting a nourishing meal on the table, mending jeans or sewing a skirt or shirt. We didn't have a lot of material possessions, but we sure had a lot of love, and I thank God for the lessons I learned from my parents.

God requires us to be good stewards of what he has given us. Here are some practical ways to help accomplish that goal.

1. Make a budget: make note of fixed and variable monthly expenses; be honest about *wants* and *needs*
   a. Fixed expenses include mortgage or rent, insurance, taxes, savings, tithes
   b. Variable expenses include food, utilities, clothing, vehicles, gasoline, entertainment

2. Shop wisely
   a. Study weekly grocery ads and make menus around sale items
   b. Use coupons
   c. Buy food on sale and freeze to use later
   d. Buy children's clothing on sale
   e. Christmas shop throughout the year instead of buying gifts all at one time
   f. Compare prices in different stores

3. Alternative ways to save
   a. Buy nice things found at garage sales
   b. Grow a garden and freeze or can what you grow
   c. Sew clothing for the family
   d. Exchange babysitting with friends
   e. Enjoy a movie/popcorn night at home
   f. Check out free museums
   g. Take a picnic to a local park instead of buying "fast food"

4. Savings: Always save some amount from each paycheck.

5. Credit: Always pay off the total balance of every credit card every month.

THANK GOD
FOR MY CHILDHOOD

My folks were poor
As they could be
When I was born
In thirty-three.

The Great Depression
Spread across the land,
So we had to live on
What was on hand.

Three big brothers
I already had,
One older sister
And a great Mom and Dad.

A good education
My folks were not given,
So they had to work hard
To scratch out a living.

But the really good life
They knew how to live—
Their time and their love
They knew how to give.

Now my Mom had a way
Of using her time
And making things stretch
On a very thin dime.

We lived on a farm
So our food was all grown—
And we gathered the wood
That heated our home.

We grew the potatoes
The corn, cabbage and greens,
The onions, tomatoes,
The carrots and beans.

The potatoes we bagged—
Put the carrots in sand—
The fruits and vegetables
Were carefully canned.

The cellar was filled
With jars all in rows,
There was plenty to feed us
Through the long winter snows.

The cows, pigs and chickens
Gave us our meat—
With eggs, meat and cream
There was plenty to eat.

Taking lunch to the hayfield
Was done with great care,
Lots of good food to eat—
Mom had it right there.

All of this work
Was a family affair;
When we canned or dressed chickens,
Each one did their share.

Ten years I was baby—
Then two more brothers arrived,
But I do not remember
Ever feeling deprived.

And then came the war—
Again, "we must save,"
My big brothers marched off,
The situation was grave.

Rationing came and
We must save for the war—
Sugar, gas, shoes and tires,
I'm sure there were more.

Our clothes were all made
From feed sacks those days,
More lessons were learned
In so many ways.

I begged my Mother:
"Please, let me sew."
The project she'd give,
Little did I know.

She returned from the bedroom
I'm sure she said, "Please."
A big stack of blue jeans
With holes in the knees.

Now back in those days
Holes weren't the style,
I didn't stop sewing
'Til I'd patched the whole pile.

I made shirts and pajamas
For my two little brothers—
Dresses, blouses and skirts,
Tea towels and others.

The shopping each week
Was carefully planned
'Cause you only could spend
The money on hand.

There are so many ways
To save a few bucks—
It's good planning and hard work—
It's not all just luck.

I thank God for my parents
Who were devoted to each other,
They worked very hard being
A good Father and Mother.

They taught us good ethics—
Not to cheat, steal or lie—
And that will stay with me
'Til the day that I die.

They taught us the things
We needed to know,
That hard work is rewarding,
How to cook and sew.

I think of them often
Even tho' they're both dead,
They prepared us all well
For what was ahead.

We're teaching our children
For today and tomorrow
How to live their life fully
In both joy and in sorrow.

Our daily responsibility
We must never shirk,
We should play with them often,
But "they must learn to work."

They must see in our lives
God's word every day,
Know the way of salvation
And know how to pray.

You can't fool your kids
If you don't pay your tithes,
If you cheat on your neighbor
Or tell your boss lies.

They learn while they're little
How to be a good husband or wife.
What you're teaching them now
Will stay with them for life.

We must carefully teach them
Good stewards to be—
The lessons most remembered
Are the ones they can see.

So, Lord, give us wisdom,
What we should do every day,
And when they ask questions
To know what to say.

I remember one time
When my children were small—
About ten in the morning,
A neighbor came to call.

The toys were all scattered
All over the floor
And I was embarrassed
As I went to the door.

She spoke words of wisdom
I never forgot—
In raising my children,
It helped me a lot.

She said, "A hundred years from now,
The world will not know
Your living room this morning
Was not fit to show.

But in raising your children
They'll be able to tell
What's really important,
So you better do well."

So I look back at childhood
And I thank God above—
I was born to a family
That knew how to show love.

Herman Arent.
circa 1938

Elaine and Eldora.
circa 1938

Dad on one of his many horses
in front of the Arent ranch.

༄ MY DAD ༄

Now I choke up a little
When I think of my Dad.
He was the most loving father
A kid ever had.

He'd come in from the field,
Toss me up in the air—
And when I came down,
He'd catch me with care.

He'd hug me so tight,
"Just fits," he would say.
I knew that he loved me,
It just was his way.

When we were real sick,
He'd hold us so tight,
Or he'd sit up and rock us
Far into the night.

I remember him saying
When I was sick in bed,
"I wish I could be there,
Sick in your stead."

We all went to the barn
'Til the chores were all done,
All the animals fed,
The cows milked one by one.

Dad filled all this time
With tales from the past,
Mixed in words of wisdom—
All our lives would sure last.

While milking the cows
Or driving the car,
He'd sing songs from the past
Or he'd point out a star.

The boys were all taught
How to make the farm run.
And Dad had a way
Of making that fun.

How to work on a tractor
Or mend up a fence—
Or when driving the car,
How to use only good sense.

Dad always had time
To take with him a kid,
And to carefully teach
Everything that he did.

For every child that he knew,
He always had time
For a hug and a kiss—
Or he'd spend his last dime.

His life was too short,
That part makes me sad,
But it was my privilege
To have him as Dad.

⌒ AS WE WALK ⌒
ON LIFE'S WAY

Eldora, Sharon, and Jack, 1987

This poem was written for Sharon Fregon, administrator at Cimarron, Kansas, after she was diagnosed with MS (multiple sclerosis). It was presented at her retirement party in 1987.

When doors open and close
As we walk on life's way,
The Lord in his mercy
Directs us each day.

In Cimarron, Kansas,
Right on Main Street,
There was a big challenge
We all would soon meet.

De-licensed, neglected—
Unkempt and rundown,
Robbed and forgotten—
The shame of the town.

The nursing home sat there
In all its despair—
Just waiting for someone
To take time to care.

A lady that lived there
Drove by each day,
Not really on purpose,
Her home was that way.

"Lord, help those poor folks,"
Each day she would pray,
"Involvement's the secret,"
She heard the Lord say.

Surely not me—
For what can I do?
I can go and I'll pray,
But I'll need some help, too.

Lord, send us a man
Who's naïve least in part,
Who has the right motives
And a really good heart.

"Ah," said the Lord,
"There's this man that I know—
Who loves a good challenge;
I'll get him to go."

So Cimarron came on
To be number five,
It took all the rest
Just to help it survive.

Now Sharon jumped in
And rose to the task,
She was beginning to see
Her prayers answered at last.

It took lots of hard work—
Meetings, budgets and tears;
For the place just to break even
Took quite a few years.

But with all of the bad times,
There were always some good,
Sharon made them or found them
As all of us should.

There are a good many other things
I could mention right here—
Like dinners with fire alarms
And a brown teddy bear.

The long trip to China,
We recall with delight,
We had fun all the day
And most of the night.

Problems just seem to vanish
When Sharon is there,
Even the small things,
Like no clothes to wear.

In her positive way,
As we know Sharon would,
She confided one day,
"My legs don't work like they should."

Other symptoms existed
And she did have some fear;
When she went to the doctor,
Just what she would hear.

After searching around,
The diagnosis came;
The doctors agreed
M.S. was its name.

If this came to me,
Would I pout? Would I cry?
Would I say, "Why me Lord?
My life's over, just let me die."

Not Sharon for sure!
She bounced back like a ball,
For her faith was in God—
An inspiration for all.

She's accepted the challenge,
Without any fuss,
As part of life's roadmap
God makes each of us.

Her great sense of humor
Will help her each day
To overcome obstacles
Placed in her way.

To the Cimarron Home,
She has been a big part;
To all us who know her,
She has touched every heart.

At VHS meetings,
We'll miss you so much;
One thing's not an option:
You must stay in touch.

᥯ JIM MABREY ᥯
FAREWELL PARTY

I wrote this farewell for Jim Mabrey, our first Vetter Health Services (VHS) accountant. We gave him a mop and bucket as a reminder of when the office was flooded and we had to clean up the mess.

Jim Mabrey, 1985

You started your profession
On life's long road
When God sent you our way
To lighten the load.

You've answered all questions
With uttermost care;
Each time we needed you,
We found you right there.

You've kicked the printer
To make it work right,
You've worked all the day
And sometimes all of the night.

You may find the tasks
In the future are varied,
Whether you're single
Or find yourself married.

This gift's a reminder
Of a piece of your past,
A job that you helped with
Each time you hoped was the last.

When the water in the office
Just wouldn't stop,
You jumped in and helped
When we gave you a mop.

We don't even question
You'll be a success—
Because with each challenge
You'll give it your best.

We'll all really miss you
As part of our team,
But we wish you God's best
As you pursue your new dream.

✧ GOD'S GIFT ✧
OF FRIENDSHIP

The Frey Family: Chet, Carol,
Michelle, Mikki, Mindy, and Matthew

Our dear friends, Chet and Carol Frey, purchased Heritage of Geneva when Jack and I purchased Heritage of Fairbury from Wayne Field, 1975. This poem was read at their farewell party at a Vetter Health Services (VHS) conference in Colorado, 1988.

Our friendship goes back
How far, I can't tell;
The night we first met you,
I remember it well.

Little did we dream
When we met you that night
That you would become
Such a part of our life.

Home from the Army,
Chet and Carol were coming,
The nursing home in Valentine
Jack was running.

Not long after that,
When our lives settled down,
We found ourselves living
All in the same town.

Your families all welcomed us
With wide open arms,
And our kids dearly loved
Being out on your farms.

The rides on the horses,
The walks by the creek,
We were always together
With plenty to eat.

Sometimes you'd drop in,
And dinner we'd cook,
But most of the nights
We spent playing Rook.

We stayed up and played
Just as long as we were able,
'Til it seems someone's cards
Would fall on the table.

Seems like the guys
Won more than their share;
And when Carol had had it,
She got up from her chair.

A frustration dance
On the trailer house floor—
And then we all sat down
And played Rook some more.

Now, friends we had found
Whose lives we could share;
In the good and the bad times,
They really did care.

Denny's bike accident
Out on the park hill,
What a bad looking face,
I remember it still.

A sick little boy
We had in those years—
But the Freys were right there
To share in our fears.

Now the summer flew by,
And so did the fall,
We moved to a house,
The Freys helped, I recall.

Then to the Freys' house,
A new blessing came,
Straight down from Heaven,
Michelle was her name.

We cuddled and loved her
And held her each day,
Not knowing the future
We'd soon move away.

Chet worked at the post office
Day after day,
"My job's not fulfilling,"
Is what Chet would say.

Running a nursing home
Is not a bad life—
It's kinda a ministry
For you and your wife.

Chet decided to try it
As God opened the door.
That was the beginning
Of what God had in store.

So the changes were made
With very little fanfare,
The Vetters were gone,
Chet and Carol stayed there.

Leaving the Freys
Really made us feel sad
Because they were the best friends
We had ever had.

Our move to Omaha
Was quite an ordeal,
I lived with my Mother—
Got the kids into school.

I remember the time
When our car didn't run,
Chet and Carol brought theirs
And they got by with one.

Finally to Omaha,
And we were moved in,
But we couldn't help missing
Our very best friends.

Then the day came
When Jack needed a man,
Freys move to Geneva
Was part of the plan.

A while after that,
By Jack's boss, he was told:
"Three of the nursing homes
Just have to be sold."

Wayne Field was sought out
Because cash he could pay,
I remember it well
It was a very sad day.

Chet stayed on in Geneva
And worked for this man.
Each day gaining favor
It was part of "God's plan."

Then came the news—
To our great surprise—
The Frey family
Was growing in size.

Sweet little Mindy
Then came into their home,
Making Michelle
No longer alone.

Two years after that,
There were three little girls.
When Mikki arrived
With her dimples and curls.

Now Chet had worked hard
And became Wayne's good friend,
Hard work and good ethics
Pays off in the end.

In seventy-four,
It was kinda late fall,
Wayne made Chet an offer,
Chet gave Jack a call:

"Come sit with me, Jack,
As we go over this deal;
As Wayne makes me an offer
Let me know how you feel."

Now isn't it fun
What God has in store
If we only will trust him
And walk through the door.

To sell off his homes,
Wayne had a great plan:
"I won't sell to a chain—
But I'll help a young man."

The young men and women,
He would carefully choose,
But he'd make them a deal
That they couldn't refuse.

Now Chet's reputation
Was that of pure gold,
So before Wayne would leave,
Geneva was sold.

So before that fall day
Would come to an end,
Chet had worked out the deal
With his boss and his friend.

Then Wayne said to Jack
When Chet's deal was through,
"The same deal on Fairbury
I'll work out with you."

All this was done
Without very much fuss,
And again the Freys' friendship
Had really blessed us.

Now the years that would follow,
We'd work night and day;
When a few winks were needed,
At Freys' house, we'd stay.

God's blessings were good,
With still more to come,
One thing was still missing
Chet wanted a son.

Their prayers would be answered
All in God's good time
When Matthew arrived
In seventy-nine.

Now the years that would follow
Were full as could be,
But we all made the effort
Each other to see.

Then Chet became restless
With all the State's fuss—
After thinking it over,
He then would call us.

So a deal on Geneva
Chet and Jack would soon fix,
And Geneva came on
In late eighty-six.

Isn't it interesting
That in God's great plan,
That if we just let him,
He uses a man.

Seems we helped you get there,
And you helped us get here,
And we've stayed best of friends
For twenty-plus years.

Many friends they have come
Just as fast they have went;
But when God brought us together,
It was no accident.

As we stop here a moment
For a view of the past—
We thank God for a friendship
That really did last.

As we look to the future,
To what God has in store,
We ask for his blessings—
You deserve them and more.

More time together
We'd all like to spend,
But friendships like ours
We won't ever let end.

We could look this world over
'Til the day that we die
And not find better friends
Than Chet & Carol Frey.

BERNIE & SUSIE

Bernie and Susie Dana

I woke up this morning
Thinking of you
And praying that God
Will see you both through.

He knows every hair
On your head, it is true;
And each step that you take,
He's always with you.

To the Lord, I am asking
That your fears will all cease,
And into its place
God will drop in his peace.

Sometimes I know
I don't pray as I should,
And then I'm reminded
That God is so good.

We want you to know
That we love you so much,
And we'll both stand behind you
And in God put our trust.

ᴄᴄ MY VALENTINE ᴅᴅ

Finding the right valentine
Is always so hard,
So I'll write you a note
And not look for a card.

My name's on the checkbook,
A nice house, a new car,
Everything I could ask for,
You're the greatest by far.

But those things aren't eternal,
They'll be gone like a dart,
But the things I love most
Are what's deep in your heart.

Eldora and Jack on a date, 1952

It's great both knowing Jesus,
The Savior of souls,
But I'm so glad that God made us
With the same Christian goals.

Your great heart for missions
Is such a part of your life,
I thank God that he let me
Share that part as your wife.

The reasons I love you
Would fill pages galore,
Then I'd read them all over
And there still would be more.

After all of these years,
I love you much more
Than the day we were wed
In mid-fifty-four.

When I look at tomorrow—
As sometimes I do—
There's nothing but sunshine
Because I have you.

I'll love you always,
Eldora

Eldora

ɛʕ MEMORIES ɜʢ

Eldora with Irene and Bernie Correll
in Hawaii 1974

Irene and Bernie

Written in 1995 for our dear friends,
Bernie and Irene Correll, for their 50th
Wedding Anniversary Book.

We've known each other for many years,
Had lots of fun and shed some tears.
The Ainsworth church would be the place
You'd raise your kids and pray for grace.

In sixty-one the Vetters came,
The church would never be the same—
With Denny crying on the stairs
And Vicki crawling through the chairs.

In early summer of sixty-two,
The station books you made me do.
Later on that year, a baby came,
The whole church's baby, Todd was his name.

We saw your daughter more than you
As the love-bug hatched and grew and grew.
Once in a while, some time we took,
We'd all sit down and play some Rook.

When my Dad died in sixty-four,
Bernie was the first one at the door.
He let me know how much he cared,
The love for Dad that we all shared.

Sixty-five would bring lots of change—
Bernie's new job seemed sorta strange.
There were showers, plans and many things,
Our families came together with wedding rings.

One day over coffee as you spoke,
Bernie's suggestion Jack took as a joke.
"A nursing home administrator you should be."
Jack quickly responded, "You're crazy, not me!"

Not long after that it would really come true,
Jack would be an administrator working with you.
We always had lots of fun together
In sunny Hawaii and stormy Christmas weather.

Once hiding Sugar, not being real nice,
Locked ourselves out, not once—but twice!
You came, spent the weekend, stayed at a motel;
While we waited together for Todd to get well.

There were ski trips and camping with lunches by lakes,
We'd all get together on our vacation breaks.
Your kids, our kids, and the grandkids we shared,
It's nice to have friends we knew really cared.

The years have passed—altogether too fast—
We thank God for a friendship that really did last.
On this 50th Anniversary, we give you our love;
May God continue to bless you as he smiles from above.

Love, Eldora & Jack

Virgle Vetter at work. circa 1990

*Virgle, Neva, Jack, and
Getha Vetter. circa 1944*

Virgle at home, 1973

Virgle with grandkids, 1973

The Vetter Family
back row: *Getha, Jack, Joani*
front row: *Neva and Virgle*
Virgle and Neva's 60th Anniversary, 1993

ᥫᥣ A TRIBUTE ᥣᥫ
TO VIRGLE VETTER

This was written for my father-in-law and read at his funeral
service at Bassett Assembly of God Church, Bassett, Nebraska,
December 22, 1997.

I recall our first meeting
In late fifty-one
As I bashfully stood
With his only son.

I remember thinking
They looked way too young,
How could they possibly have
A nearly grown son.

Virgle was quiet, reserved
And shy from the start—
But before very long,
He had a place in my heart.

The day finally came
When I married their son,
As one of the kids
I soon would become.

Then came the day
That first grandson was born,
We lived at their house,
Up at five every morn!

Virgle would hold him and goo-goo
Night, morning and noon;
Put his thumb in his mouth;
Give him coffee from a spoon.

Then there was Vicki—
Long before she was two,
He'd taught all the verses
Of *Little Boy Blue*.

There were Lori and Patti
And Todd in a row,
And Grandpa was part
Of their lives; don't you know.

Then there was Vonnie,
A frail little gal;
Through all of her problems,
He was her best pal.

Then came Gary and Virgie,
Along with Shelly and Jen,
His eyes would light up
When they would walk in.

They remember the pickup—
Or the bumps they would toss
While Grandpa was humm'n
The Old Rugged Cross.

Each year in the spring,
The ranch was the place,
With Grandma and Grandpa,
They all loved the space.

The work in the hay field
Was long days that were hot—
But from this special Grandpa,
They all learned a lot.

They learned on the job
You must never shirk—
Get an honest day's pay
For an honest day's work.

They loved him a lot,
As most grandchildren do;
For the things that he taught them,
They respected him, too!

Be honest; work hard;
Give from the heart, not for fame—
That your greatest possession
Is a good, honest name.

The ranch and the cattle
Were a big part of his life,
But he truly did love
His family and wife.

The folks at the feed yard
Have all been so nice
As Virgle stopped in
Every day, once or twice!

The sale barns will miss him,
They all called him by name;
They'll continue their auctions,
But they won't be the same.

The great grandkids were special
As they stood by his bed,
His eyes would light up
As he patted their head.

His three lovely children
Were the pride of his life,
He loved them all dearly
And also his wife.

We'll miss him a lot,
And that makes us all sad,
But it's been our privilege
To know him as "DAD"!

∽ RETIREMENT ∽

I wrote this poem to share with family and friends at my retirement party from Vetter Health Services (VHS), December 1998.

Eldora and Jack Vetter, 1998

My co-workers, my friends
And my family so dear,
Can it really be possible
That retirement is here?

A real balancing act,
That's been my life:
Kids, church, and the office,
Plus being Jack's wife.

We've talked on the phone,
Or I saw you each day—
You are part of my life,
And I hope that will stay!

All the friendships we've formed,
You each have your niche;
But we'll pass the torch forward
Without even a glitch.

To my family so dear—
You've always been there;
I trust in the future,
There'll be more time to share.

Thank you for coming
To my party tonight.
Your presence here with us
Has been my delight.

It's not my intention
That this be the end,
I'll still be around
And you'll still be my friend.

ҩ THANK YOU ҩ
FOR 25 YEARS

Jack and Eldora Vetter, 2000

This poem was written and personally presented by Eldora at Vetter Health Services (VHS) 25th Anniversary, 2000.

To our Mom and our Dads who've gone on before,
As you stand and look down from the golden shore.
We hope you are pleased with what you now see—
That we're the adults you hoped we would be.

You always were there to show us the way.
The things that you taught us still guide us today.
We miss you a lot, but your memory lives on.
We think of you often, even though you are gone.

To our Mom who is with us and joins us today,
Who loves and encourages and remembers to pray.
We thank you for coming, this party to share,
Not just for tonight, you've always been there!

We thank you, our children, for all the good years,
You've been such a blessing, with very few tears.
We could trust you to go and do as we asked
Or to stay home alone or to finish each task!

The spouses you brought us—we love them all three—
They are more than just in-laws, they've become family.
Then there's the grandchildren, we love you each one—
And we're sure looking forward to more years of fun.

To Wayne Field, we say, "Thank You," for opening the door,
For the chances you took in late seventy-four.
Fairbury's been a great home from beginning to end,
You were a good mentor and have become a great friend!

To all of the owners of the homes we have bought:
For that opportunity and that trust, we thank you a lot.
In every location we've stood not alone,
We would not be there now had you not started that Home.

To all our employees as we have joined hands:
You've hung in there, right with us, to meet the demands.
You've come early, stayed late, to get the work done.
For being part of our team, we thank you each one.

To our Quality Partners, a "Thank You," we say
For being willing and ready to serve us each day.
In your work, as in ours, there's a goal that we share,
To be the best that we can and give quality care.

To our friends and our loved ones whose lives that we share:
In the good times and bad times, you've always been there!
We treasure your friendship, both future and past,
We've been friends for years, so we know that will last.

To our Heavenly Father who is Lord of our life,
As we started this journey as husband and wife:
For the doors you have opened, and closed a few too,
The strength and the courage to see each day through.

For the blessings you give us with every new day,
For the failures and challenges that get in the way;
For with them comes knowing we must trust in you,
To give us the wisdom for each thing that we do.

The future is with you, as it has been in the past.
Knowing only what's done for you will last!
We thank you, Dear Lord, for being with us each day,
Please be with each of our guests as they go on their way!

Arent Family—
back row: *Iloe, Bonnie, and Leslie*
front row: *Mary, Linda, Julie, and Helen.*
circa 1961

Iloe and Leslie Arent

HAPPY 50TH ANNIVERSARY
LES & ILOE

Written for my second brother, Leslie, and his wife, Iloe, for their 50th Wedding Anniversary, January 31, 2002.

I was in on *"the secret,"* the date had been set,
We'd stop off in Valentine, a few things to get.
A new dress for Iloe and maybe some rings,
I don't remember it all—may have been some more things.

To South Dakota we'd go, a judge we would find,
The ceremony was performed and the papers were signed.
Didn't take very long for you to become man and wife,
And you started your journey for a very full life.

Later on in that year, a sweet bundle came,
Blue eyes and blond hair, Helen, her name.
Time quickly passed and there were two little girls
When Mary arrived with red hair and curls.

I came to Rock County in mid fifty-four,
Being near the same town we'd see you lots more!
Then Julie arrived to make three little girls,
She had big dancing eyes and some little white curls.

The girls were so cute as they all sat in a row.
We'd see them a lot when to church we would go.
But that would all change to answer Uncle Sam's call,
But we would return the following fall.

Little Linda was born the 26th of September—
Jack left for France, how well I remember.
We'd see lots of each other for several more years,
We shared good times, bad times, laughter and tears.

We had Denny and Vicki when Bonnie arrived,
Now we had two and you guys had five!
We'd oft get together, let the children all play
At your house or our house, we'd all spend the day.

You called us one day, "bring your camera and film,"
A bobcat you'd caught—wanted some pictures of him.
We all were so busy—worked hard every day—
We'd all stay in touch without much time to play!

Then you guys got restless, decided to go
Away to Wisconsin with its trees, cold and snow.
We'll never forget the day of your sale,
It was snowing real hard—the wind blowing a gale!

Dad came to the sale—had walked much of the way—
And Jack milked the cows for a couple of days.
You stayed at our house for a few days or so;
When the weather cleared up, away you would go.

The years that would follow—you seemed far away—
Sure different than seeing you almost every day.
There were hunting trips, funerals, anniversaries and such,
But with the mail and the phone, we did stay in touch.

To Wisconsin, however, we'd manage to come,
All the kids were delighted, did they ever have fun.
They'd go to the barn, build forts in the hay,
They'd play through the night and into the next day.

Then the kids all grew up, and each one went their way,
Giving the Moms and the Dads more time to play.
Light for Lost Convention was always a treat,
We'd both travel a distance, was a great place to meet.

We'd all meet together with one common goal:
To raise money for missions and the reaching of souls.
It's so good to have family you can share your faith with,
Serving God with each other is truly a gift!

We appreciate your faithfulness to God every day
You've served him steadfastly all of the way.
Iloe, we love you—for your great servant's heart,
You're always right there doing more than your part.

You've blessed many churches in the past fifty years,
God has faithfully kept you through triumphs and fears.
We now place the future into God's hands,
Knowing he already has every day planned!

May each day that now follows be cheery and bright
And each step that you take bring you only delight.
We wish you God's best for the rest of your days.
We Love you a lot—in so many ways.

Love, Jack & Eldora

⋅⋅⋅ MY BABY BROTHER ⋅⋅⋅

*Written and read for my youngest brother, Lyle Arent, at his
retirement party, May 2004.*

How well I remember
The day you were born:
The fifth of December,
A cold winter morn.

Then you came home
With Daddy and Mother,
I'd soon get to know
My new baby brother.

My two little brothers
I loved from the start.
From that day to this,
A special place in my heart.

I learned to change diapers—
Get you ready to go,
Mom took me along
As sitter, you know.

Alvin and Lyle Arent. circa 1945

Lyle and Alvin. circa 1952

'New Boots' Lyle and Alvin. circa 1952

Jack Vetter with Bob, Herman, Lyle, and Alvin Arent, 1951

Lyle and Glenna with children Lora Lee and Stacy. circa 1975

I had some pet names:
"Inky-Binky" was one.
You were my baby brother
Sometimes more like a son.

When I'd come home from school,
If it had been a long day,
My mother would tell me,
"Just take the boys out and play."

We made dams in the water
And roads in the sand,
Our toys back in those days
Were made with our hands.

My big brothers teased me,
"The Runt" was Jack's name.
When you announced his arrival,
That ended their game.

Then came the time
When I would leave home—
Had jobs and a husband
And kids of my own.

The years quickly passed,
Then we moved back to town,
You were in high school
And always around.

My children all loved you;
You were like no other,
You were more than an uncle,
More like their big brother.

You always had time
For a bucking horse ride,
Walk the floor with a baby,
Or just take them outside.

There were 409 cars
And girls all around—
But somehow you managed
To keep your feet on the ground.

There were groundings and spats,
Everything under the sun—
But when it came time to choose,
You picked the "right one!"

There were weddings and babies,
Moves in all kinds of weather,
But we always made time
To just get together.

Our kids are part yours,
And yours are part mine—
To be part of their lives,
We both always found time!

The Omaha years—
We were always together,
When both you and Jack
Worked for Bethesda.

There were trips to the mountains
With trailers and bikes—
Mostly it was fun—
But sometimes a few "Yikes!"

Your job kept you busy,
But when it brought you our way,
You'd drop in for the night,
'Twas a good place to stay.

We found our nests empty
Before we could know,
But there were still things to do
And places to go!

The cruises together,
We could both write a book,
We still have places to go,
So we'll continue to look.

In good times and sad times
I know you'll be there—
As we look to the future,
Our lives we will share!

I'm so glad Mom and Dad
Made plans to have you,
'Cause all the rest of us kids
Really needed you too!

Daddy's life was too short,
That still makes me sad
But you missed the most—
You were only a lad.

You stepped up to the plate,
You were so good to Mother;
When the going got tough,
We could count on each other.

If Daddy could see
The man you've become,
He'd be so proud
To call you his son.

I hope we can spend
Even more time with each other,
'Cause you always will be
"My baby brother!"

I love you, Bud!!

~ DALTON ~

Dalton Dean Vetter,
kindergarten graduation

Written about Dalton and his kindergarten school year.
Presented at kindergarten graduation in April 2006.

Dalton is six, and he sure is all boy!
He has always loved life—and brings everyone joy

His smile is contagious, he likes so many things,
He finds it exciting to dance and to sing.

He loves riding bikes, roller skating and skiing,
Playing rescue heroes and going sight seeing!

He'll play dolly with sister or sit down for tea,
Life's always exciting for Dalton, you see.

He swims in the pool and plays at the park,
Digs in the sandbox from dawn until dark.

He likes to play soccer, to camp and to fish,
He loves to eat ice cream from a cone or a dish.

He loves jigsaw puzzles, likes cards and board games,
When kids are around, he knows all of their names.

A whole new adventure for Dalton this year—
It's called kindergarten, can't believe it is here.

Learning writing and reading and some arithmetic,
He became quite creative with popsicle sticks.

His units included leaves, apples, water and nests,
The moon and the sun, rocks and also insects.

There were lessons on animals—from the farm, water and zoo—
The strange ones from Africa and about dinosaurs too!

He learned about maps and a globe that is round,
How to follow a map and find the next town.

The field trips were exciting, we all had great fun,
Dalton wanted to know when will be the next one?

School will bring its excitement—its achievements and strife—
But there's one thing for certain—Dalton will always love life!

SPECIAL OCCASIONS

⌒ VETTERS GO ⌒
THE EXTRA MILE

This was written for a competition between teams at a Vetter Health Service (VHS) conference. It was intended to be used as a rap-style song.

It seems a year has come and gone
Since we made up our last year's song
Now some of us are very new
But we can learn a lot from you

You have us all together now
I'm sure you hope to teach us how
When you come out to visit us
This is what you'll find—we trust

> *Vetters go the extra mile*
> *And always do it with a smile*
> *We stand out from all the rest*
> *Because we are the very best*

The grass outside is cut and green
The home inside is sparkling clean
Someone will greet you at the door
As you walk on our shiny floor

Our staff's well trained and happy too
They work together just like glue
Our residents are clean and neat
And sitting in their favorite seat

Vetters go the extra mile
And always do it with a smile
We stand out from all the rest
Because we are the very best

The food we serve is always great
And served on time—we're never late
Or if that day they're sick in bed
We'll serve it in their room instead

The home is all in good repair
We even cut and fix their hair
The laundry done and in the drawer
And extra groceries all in store

Vetters go the extra mile
And always do it with a smile
We stand out from all the rest
Because we are the very best

Our nursing care is all first rate
When we are surveyed by the state
Deficiencies—they wouldn't dare
Because we give the finest care

The budget goals that we all set
You will see they've all been met
Our books are always done on time
And Jack is pleased with the bottom line

Vetters go the extra mile
And always do it with a smile
We stand out from all the rest
Because we are the very best

AS CHRISTMAS DRAWS NEAR

We stop for a moment
As Christmas draws near,
To ponder our favorite
Time of the year.

We all are as busy
As people can be—
We must wrap the gifts
And then trim the tree.

As we hurry here
And hurry there,
Let's not forget
To take time to share.

When we ponder a gift,
It's not the amount—
That's not what Christmas
Is all about.

The first Christmas gift
Was one of great love,
When God sent Jesus
To us from above.

When you help the old lady
With a trembling hand,
Or you give a big hug
To the little old man.

Your gifts of love,
Every day you give out;
Now, that's what Christmas
Is all about.

We thank you at Christmas
And all through the year,
As your gentle hands
Give out gifts of good cheer.

Today as you walk through
The halls of the home,
Remember the ones
That may be all alone.

Give them the gift
That only you can,
That lonely old lady
Or cross little man.

Sometimes we wish
We had money to share
When often the best gift
Is just being there.

If we give of our love
And don't limit the amount,
We'll all learn together
What Christmas is about.

We send you our love,
And this is the reason:
Christmastime is
The most special season.

⤳ DIME JARS ⤳

Written and pasted on our church's "Dimes for Souls" jars, encouraging the ladies of Women's Ministries to save their dimes for missions.

A few dimes a week
Is all that we ask.
So put your dimes in,
Let's get with the task.

You won't even miss them
As you save two or three,
God will make up the difference,
Just trust him and see.

If we all work together,
We can soon reach our goals.
As month after month
We save *Dimes for Souls.*

⟋ PASTORS ARE SPECIAL ⟍

This poem was written and sent along with a letter from Cornerstone Church to alert the congregation of a special offering that was going to be collected for the pastors, Christmas 1988.

Our Pastors are special,
We're sure that you know,
But often our gratitude
We're quite slow to show.

We take them for granted
A lot of the year,
But let us not do that
As Christmas draws near.

The first Christmas gift
Was the greatest of love—
When God gave us Jesus
From heaven above.

On this Sunday morning,
The eighteenth of December,
We'll take up an offering,
Our Pastors to remember.

So bring your love offering
And/or a card of love, too;
And let's let them know
We appreciate what they do.

∽ BERNIE ∾

This was written as a thank you to Bernie Dana in 1989.

I looked and I looked
And I couldn't find
The sort of a card
We both had in mind.

We wanted to say
"We appreciate you,"
And all of the things
You so willingly do.

To find the right man
Was simply a must,
With a great deal of knowledge
And one we could trust.

You help us to see
The things we should do,
And set up a plan
To see them all through.

Your experience, your standards
Your Christian principles, too;
In both business and friendship
We love and appreciate you.

CHRISTMAS GIFT CLUES

This was the year Mitch was learning to fly the airplane. At Christmas, we had drawn names and were supposed to give funny or gag gifts. I decided to buy Mitch an airplane urinal as a gag gift and wrote this poem to go with it.

What's in this box—you'll never guess
It could keep you out—of one big mess!

I'm something—you don't have in store
But if I'm needed—you can't ignore!

I'm not found in most sale books
Nor am I known for my good looks

I can be used by gal or guy—
On the ground—or in the sky

New experiences are real exciting
Which could make me—even more inviting

You almost never think of me
Unless I'm needed desperately!

Your fancy friends I won't impress
Unless they are in great distress

I'm seldom used because of pride!
But when I'm needed, you can't hide.

Now if you take good care of me
I'll be your friend—I guarantee

I've given you most every clue
Now you can guess what and who!

⟡ I'LL BE YOUR FRIEND ⟡

This poem was given to the boys, Den, Todd, and Tony, along with a Walkman Radio for Christmas.

I'll be your friend from dusk to dawn—
Even when you mow the lawn.

I'll be your friend in sun or fog—
And even when you walk the dog.

I'll be your friend as you roller-blade—
And when Nebraska games are played.

I'll be your friend as you hunt and walk—
And when you plain don't want to talk.

I'll be your friend most anywhere—
When you're mad or glad or just don't care.

If you just take good care of me—
I'll work for you almost cost free.

When I'm not with you, put me away—
And I'll be your friend day after day.

But if you leave me lying around
In car seats or on the ground—

I won't be your friend for very long,
You'll miss my company and my song.

I'll be your friend, stay by your side—
If by these rules you just abide.

Love,
Mom

ᒣ ESPECIALLY FOR YOU... ᒧ

As part of our Christmas gift each year, Jack and I invite our children and grandchildren to join us for a family ski week in Colorado. In 1995, we presented the gift in the form of a poem.

This is a special invitation just for you
To join in the fun—with the whole Vetter crew.

The date is in April the first weekend you know
The place is the condo—where we always go!

We'll ride the lift up—and ski it back down
When the last run is finished, we'll hurry to town!

All tired and hungry—the food will taste good
Because it is there—we'll eat more than we should.

The hot tub is the next place—we'll all go for fun
Get your swimmin' suit on—and we'll make a run!

We'll play and we'll soak—'til we have wrinkled skin
We must then all get out—so the next group can get in!

There'll be videos, colors, pencils, papers and games—
Then will come bedtime—we'll start through the names!

Jace, Ty, Shaye and Caleb, we'll tuck you in tight—
Revonna, Tristan and Jacob—to bed for the night.

Where will we all sleep? There will be room for all!
Those in the loft—must take care not to fall.

We must all be quiet! So Grammy can sleep,
Or she'll be crabby tomorrow (there'll be nothing to eat!)

There'll be lodging and food, lift tickets and fun
So please come along and join everyone.

You may ski, shop, watch TV and go at your own pace
One thing to remember, keep a smile on your face.

Lots of Love,
Grammy and Papa

⸱ BERNIE & ZAIGA ⸱

Zaiga and Tom Moriarty, Jack and Eldora Vetter,
Susie and Bernie Dana

Just a little note to say
That we appreciate the way
You worked and worked
Both night and day.

Operating plans
Just aren't much fun,
It always seems
There's more to come.

But you so faithfully
Saw it through
Each time there was
More work to do.

I looked and looked
And couldn't find
A card that begins to say
What's on our mind.

So here's a
Great big thanks to you
For always being
Jack's faithful crew.

P.S.
Thanks to Susie and Tom
Who sat alone,
Wondering if you guys
Would ever come home.

Hopefully, it will
Be worth it all
As things are on course
Going into fall.

ᴄᴄ THE EIGHTH DAY! ᴄ͜ᴄ
(YOUR REQUEST FOR MORE DAYS
HAS NOW REACHED MY DESK)

This is one of the "fun things" that was ongoing at our office for quite some time. It started with Bernie and Zaiga writing a letter to Jack requesting an eighth day be added to the week. Jack responded with quotes from the Bible and reasons why an eighth day was not feasible. It went back and forth for a while and this was my contribution to the fun.

Your request for more days
Has now reached my desk,
I don't have the solution
But I'll give it my best.

As I ponder more time,
I wonder would it really pay
If somehow could be added
To each week just a day?

Eight days in each week—
That seems like a lot,
Think of the overtime
We'd pay at each spot.

We'd have to come up with
Three more shifts every day—
And all the employees
Would ask for more pay.

Thirty more nurses and staff
We'd add right away
To cover all shifts
Both at night and each day.

"We're all out of food,"
The cooks would all cry;
And the laundry would pile up
'Til it reached the sky.

The cleaning people would rush
To give it their best,
They'd get done what they could
And just leave the rest.

At all the facilities,
The people would be tired
And pressing the administrator
To get more people hired.

All the administrators
Would be pulling their hair
Trying to maintain
Vetter's quality care.

The operating plans
That are already completed
Would get pulled back in
And totally deleted.

It comes to the question:
Are we really ahead,
To give up the old week
And have eight days instead?

Another big question:
What would residents say
If we were to tell them
We've added a day?

That all looks to me
Like an awfully big mess,
Maybe the both of you
Just need a good rest.

I've considered your plight,
And the facility's too,
And here is the best thing
I can offer to you:

Take off early on Friday,
Rest both Saturday and Sunday—
Then come back all refreshed
Bright and early on Monday!

FROM THE DESK OF
"THE HIGHER
AUTHORITY"

⸺ THANK YOU! ⸺

Thank you that appeared in the paper after Jack's Dad's funeral.

To all of you
Who came to share
And let us know
How much you care:

The words, the food,
And the kind deeds
Have helped so much
With all our needs.

Your love to Virg
In many ways
Brought happiness
To all his days!

You are all so kind—
To help and give
It makes our town
A great place to live.

Thanks for being there!
The Virgle Vetter Family

☙ FOR JOANI ❧

At a leadership team meeting, we drew names and I drew my sister-in-law Joani's name. We were challenged to purchase a gift and write instructions on how it was to be used. I gave Joani a sack of little things: a pen, a calendar, a ruler, and a flower planter along with this poem.

Joani succeeded me as Director of Financial Services at Vetter Health Services (VHS), thus the poem reference to Jack, owner of VHS.

Joani Schelm

I give you this pen for when
You must draw the line.
Please note that its point
Is durable and fine.

It does not contain
One drop of red ink;
But it gives you a cap
For more time to think!

Looking closely you'll notice
It's blue and not black;
Specifically meant to allow
You some slack.

The calendar included
Is to give you more time.
The ruler is intended
To keep Jack in line!

The planter is to remind you
To take time to play,
So you'll be ready and anxious
To start each new day.

❧ NO ORDINARY BEAR ❧

Todd Vetter, 1965

This poem was written for our youngest son, Todd, for his 40th birthday. It was given to him along with his "Old Teddy Bear"—the one he loved so much as a child.

I want you to know—I'm no ordinary bear,
The threads that you see are caused from much wear.

I was high on the shelf at the Ainsworth Dime Store,
But of all the toys there—Todd wanted me more.

Mom would buy me for him—if no tears were shed
If he'd quietly lay while she put in his meds.

With his head hanging over—on the couch he would lay,
While the nose drops went in—at least three times a day.

You can tell by my hair—I was the favorite toy
And the Very Best Friend of one little boy.

Every day we took naps—and to bed every night,
We'd crawl under the covers—we'd snuggle up tight.

Each time at the hospital—from beginning to end,
I'd stay right there with him—'cause I was his friend.

Now, please carefully keep me even though I am frayed,
And remember that always—by your side I have stayed.

ABOUT THE AUTHOR

$\mathscr{E}$LDORA VETTER

$\mathscr{E}$ldora Vetter is the cofounder of Vetter Health Services (VHS) with Jack, her husband of fifty-six years. The company is committed to fulfilling their corporate mission of providing dignity in life for the elderly.

Prior to retiring from her position as Chief Financial Officer in December 1998, Eldora was one of the driving forces behind the success of the company. In the early days, she pitched in where needed, whether that was handling the interior decoration or keeping books. Today, she remains active in the company and serves on the Board of Directors.

The love and discipline of strong families helped guide Eldora and Jack on their path to discovering their mission to give the elderly a place to feel respected, secure, comfortable and happy. Both sets of Eldora's grandparents were homesteaders. Hard work kept a roof over their heads and food on the table.

This traditional work ethic evolved through the generations and gave Eldora and Jack the firm grounding and inspiration they needed to build their facilities and management.

Hard work was a given for Eldora. After graduating from high school, she worked as a secretary for attorneys in Ainsworth, Nebraska. As a newlywed in 1954, she took a position with the Bassett Chamber of Commerce—the only job she ever applied for—and later, she worked at the local bank. Opportunities always awaited her. And she was quick to seize them.

After Jack completed basic military training, they lived in Fort Polk, Louisiana; but Eldora returned to Bassett when Jack deployed overseas to France. During this time, she handled bookkeeping for Bassett's Kozy Café and the Red Robin filling station.

The Vetters moved first to Ainsworth, Nebraska, then to Valentine, Nebraska, where Eldora worked at Pine View Manor nursing home doing payroll and secretarial work.

In 1975, Jack and Eldora purchased their first facility and began a tradition of care that has endured through the years as a respected example of excellence to the profession.

Vetter Health Services (VHS) owns or manages thirty-three long-term care, assisted living, and independent living facilities in a five-state area of the Midwest with corporate offices in Elkhorn, Nebraska.

Eldora and Jack have three children: Denny, Vicki and Todd who have given them nine grandchildren and two great-grandchildren.

Eldora has a strong faith and knowledge of the Bible. She shares her writing talent through poetry for devotions, gifts, recognitions, and expressions of love to her family and friends. This book is testament to her eloquent story-telling skills through her beautiful rhymes and biblical interpretations.

Lifetime Achievement Award

When Eldora Vetter was presented with a Lifetime Achievement Award at a VHS Administrator's Conference, this heartfelt introduction was given by her staff.

*B*orn in Merrimen, Nebraska, the fifth child and second daughter to Herman and Effie Arent on September 30, 1933, Eldora Vetter grew up the daughter of a rancher and his wife—people of humble means who were kind-hearted and who cherished family.

Eldora graduated from Ainsworth High School in 1951. She married Jack on June 6, 1954, and has been his wife, friend, business partner and help mate.

They have three children—two sons and a daughter, one son-in-law and two daughters-in-law, nine grandchildren.

One of life's greatest pleasures for Eldora is to dote on her own family and others. She loves the role of mother, grandmother and friend.

- ℯ² She hugs and cuddles babies close as often as she can when they are little. According to her, they never stay infants long enough.

- ℯ² She finds joy in the antics of toddlers and loves to play learning games with them.

- ℯ² She enjoyed cooking and sitting around the camp fire in the mountains with her family and others as the kids grew up.

- ℯ² She makes incredible homemade jam and fresh bread to go with—always served with plenty of butter.

- ℯ² Christmas abounds with a house full of decorations everywhere you look, store-bought gifts that are exquisitely wrapped alongside those special garage sale finds that are wrapped in newspaper (which was often the most favorite gift of all).

Speaking of garage sales … Eldora is the greatest garage-saler of all time!

- ℯ² She loves to find that perfect birthday or Christmas gift for each member of her family at the weekly Thursday morning garage sale route.

- ℯ² She likes to stop by the office and regale her latest find for an office staffer—her second kids. She scouts out good used fun clothes and toys for their kids as well as items to furnish first dorm rooms or that new little house that they may be trying to make into a home.

- She keeps the VHS Interior Designer supplied with plenty of wall hangings, décor items, old books, doilies, and pretty things from which to choose when they are putting the final touches to a room or wing.

- She enjoys finding the deal of the century on the Ethan Allen dining room sets, along with china for the private dining rooms at the nursing homes.

At home:

- She loves to crochet doilies, bedspreads, pillow covers and lamp shades.

- Eldora is a proficient seamstress—making quilts, drapes, and clothes including her daughter Vicki's wedding dress.

- She prepares her garden in the spring—and we all benefit: roses for her home and office throughout the summer and garden produce in the fall—often by the bucket. Sometimes we even enjoy her famous lime pickles during Friday staff lunches.

- She loves to cook and bake for her family. Holiday dinners are a grand event with ironed linen, greenery and candles cascading from the center of the table that is set with fine china and crystal goblets.

- Jack and Eldora enjoy entertaining in their home. She can turn out a spectacular dinner in 45 minutes; defrosting those farm-grown New York strips from the freezer, Jack throws them on the grill while she puts the finishing touches on a meal to rival any fine restaurant's best. And the guests, often missionaries, arrive to the aroma of home-made rhubarb or apple pies, which were made ahead and frozen and go directly from the freezer to the oven, then often topped with freshly churned vanilla ice cream made with the required farm-raised eggs.

℮ These guests are occasionally overnight visitors who are always treated like family and enjoy the spacious and well-furnished guest room in the lower level.

As business owner and partner:

℮ Eldora accepted the decisions of her husband and business partner and supported him in so many ways.

℮ She brought her talents for stretching a penny to the business and often worked nights and weekends to paint a resident's room, an office, the dining room, or a day room to make their first nursing home acquisitions into a home for the residents they cared for. She "was" VHS's first interior designer.

℮ She lent her skill in bookkeeping to the company, and negotiated mortgages with local bankers.

℮ She would graciously appear at VHS conferences and on several occasions gave devotions that would move several to tears. It was characteristic of her to share a poem she had written for a special occasion with the group that was gathered.

Eldora is the epitome of an angel when it comes to sitting at someone's bedside or sharing the afternoon with a family member or friend in the surgery waiting room. She finds the fun in her own jokes, can laugh easily at the silly things she catches herself doing, and has a smile and a hug for you when you enter the room. There is always a place set for you at her dining room table if you ever find yourself in Omaha. She is everyone's friend and often a second mom.

For these reasons and more, we present Eldora with "The Lifetime Achievement Award."